IT'S ABOUT TIME

*How businesses
can save the world*
(one worker at a time)

SAFWAN SHAH

Conscious Capitalism Press
www.consciouscapitalism.org/press

Round Table Companies
Packaging, production, and distribution services
www.roundtablecompanies.com

Printed in the United States of America

First Edition: April 2019
10 9 8 7 6 5 4 3 2 1

Library of Congress Cataloging-in-Publication Data
Shah, Safwan.
It's about time: how businesses can save the world (one worker at a time)
/ Safwan Shah.—1st ed. p. cm.
ISBN Paperback: 978-1-950466-03-0
ISBN Hardcover: 978-1-950466-04-7
ISBN Digital: 978-1-950466-02-3
Library of Congress Control Number: 2019935428

Conscious Capitalism Press is an imprint of Conscious Capitalism, Inc.
The Conscious Capitalism Press logo is a trademark of Conscious Capitalism, Inc.

Round Table Companies and the RTC logo are trademarks
of Writers of the Round Table, Inc.

illustrator **Daya Mundaye**
editor **Corey Blake**
designer **Sunny DiMartino**
proofreaders **Adam Lawrence, Carly Cohen**

To the heroic business leaders who have recognized and done something to address the toxic impact of financial stress on lower-wage workers: you have my heart-filled gratitude.

Contents

Foreword by Raj Sisodia

About a year ago, when I was starting to write *The Healing Organization*, I went to a Chinese restaurant. At the end of the meal, the fortune cookie revealed the following: **"There are many ways you can be hurtful, but only one way to heal. That is through love."**

It is that simple, and that profound. Too many of us in the world of business have lost our innocence, have lost our simplicity, are no longer rooted in love and in truth. But we can get back to all of those things. It is simply a matter of awareness and intention. As one of the great souls of the modern world of business and economics, Muhammad Yunus, has said, "We've used our creative power to focus on making money—and we've done it like it's the only game in town. It's not. There's a more exciting game in town." That game is to help other people. And when those people are in the inner circle of our own business family—our employees—the joy that comes from making their lives even a little bit better is palpable and deeply gratifying.

How can we evolve our market-based economy so that it does not feel predatory, exploitative, or transactional? By creating an economy in which we joyfully and gratefully meet the real needs of our fellow living beings, rather than extracting as much out of them for ourselves as possible.

The two strongest human drives are self-interest and our profound need to care. But the *order* in which we attend to these needs matters hugely. We need to move what has been in the background to the foreground, and what has been in the foreground to the background.

What has been in the foreground has been the idea that a market economy functions well when all participants pursue their self-interest to the hilt. That means that we focus on attaining success by using our gifts to meet the needs of other people.

In the background is the idea that we need to *care* about the people whose needs we are trying to meet. To many, this is simply a pragmatic realization; if you don't care for your customers and your employees, they will soon leave you. So, you better care about them, or at least give them the *impression* that you care about them.

Caring for others can thus become a masked version of still being primarily focused on your own self-interest. You don't *really* care about them. You only care because they have money in their pocket that you want or skills in their hands and minds that you need.

We need to flip what is in the background and in the foreground. We need to lead with a sincere desire to be of service to others. Look deep within your heart to find the kind of service that will nourish you (the giver) as it will nourish the recipient.

In other words: **Be in business to express yourself and serve others, not to serve yourself and use others.**

Safwan Shah's inspiring story is a beautiful illustration of that maxim. He has started a company, PayActiv, explicitly to help heal the deep financial suffering of the most vulnerable among us.

The scale of the problem is staggering. In thirty-five years (1978–2013), worker pay in the US only increased by 10 percent. But it's actually gone down for the lower bottom 50 percent of earners. Over 90 million Americans live paycheck to paycheck, and pay close to $100 billion in financial fees and penalties. There is little buffer between them and financial ruin. According to the National Bureau of Economic Research, 50 percent of Americans have less than $400 in the bank, and would not be able to raise $2000 within thirty days in the event of an emergency of any kind. This includes tapping into friends, family, and their employers. An estimated 60 percent of American households are technically insolvent, which means that their liabilities exceed their assets. Most of them are going further into debt every year, at a time of historically low interest rates. One shudders to think of what will happen to them when interest rates normalize.

Small changes at the right time can make a huge difference. As the old proverb goes:

For want of a nail the shoe was lost.
For want of a shoe the horse was lost.
For want of a horse the rider was lost.
For want of a rider the message was lost.
For want of a message the battle was lost.
For want of a battle the kingdom was lost.

Safwan's passion is to help people move toward holistic financial wellness, getting them out of the holes that they are in, and helping them pave a more secure path to their future. His is a systems approach to healing one of the deepest and most persistent sources of suffering in our society.

Safwan is an exemplary conscious leader with a deeply healing message that needs to be heard and heeded by leaders everywhere. This book is packed with wisdom from a life wonderfully well lived, which holds out great promise for huge positive impacts to come in the years ahead.

RAJ SISODIA
F. W. Olin Distinguished Professor of Global Business and Whole Foods Market Research Scholar in Conscious Capitalism, Babson College
Cofounder and Cochairman, Conscious Capitalism, Inc.

You can resist an invading army;
you cannot resist an idea whose time has come.

VICTOR HUGO

What man actually needs is not a tensionless
state but rather the striving and struggling
for a worthwhile goal, a freely chosen task.

VIKTOR FRANKL

Perhaps the best conversationalist in the world is
the man who helps others to talk.

JOHN STEINBECK

Introduction

Time is of the essence.

Our low- to medium-wage workers are suffering. They live from paycheck to paycheck. Consequently, they can't easily recover from a tiny financial setback. As a result, they exist in a state of constant financial fragility and anguish—which in turn impacts businesses with higher worker attrition, lack of on-the-job focus, and a host of related performance drains.

Certainly, the government can act with regulation, leading to ideas such as setting a higher minimum wage or offering an earned income tax credit for relative low-wage families. Going forward, many jurisdictions can similarly be expected to experiment with new ideas such as a universal basic income. But such actions are not easy to implement and nearly always carry unanticipated and generally negative outcomes. The fact is, the best solutions to such economic challenges rarely arise from politicians but from businessmen. Businesses themselves—a free-enterprise system operating with the right sets of information—will nearly always develop a much more equitable, effective, and sustainable outcome.

But therein lies the problem: a glaring blind spot. Business leaders today are not seeing the entire picture, and because of that they are not considering all of the relevant variables. In particular, they are not paying enough attention to—they are not thinking creatively about—TIME.

Here's why they should.

Chapter One

My Own Initial Conditions

"About" Safwan: to better understand this book and its objectives, a bit more about the author

- *The "Hollywood Years," or the intersections with Tom Hanks and space flight*
- *Humble beginnings: from Pakistan to the US*
- *Pakistan: then, now, and how it happened*
- *Where's the funding? (Designing experiments for NASA and the space shuttle)*
- *My brush with poverty and abject despair*

■ ■ ■

Before we go much further, I feel it's important to put all of my cards on the table. Okay, that's not the most appropriate analogy. We're not gambling here; this isn't a showdown; there are no rules in place to determine whether my hand or yours is the better one.

This is more a case of the need for full disclosure—and, in fact, I am about to disclose far beyond what anyone might need to know to better benefit from or possibly enjoy the ramblings, recollections, and (hopefully) worthwhile insights to come. That is, in addition to a full reveal of my corporate affiliations and interests, I'm also going to share a bit of my personal background.

Full Disclosure

My background matters because, whenever you read a passage in this book, I want you to be able to make your own determination as to whether you're being informed, entertained, indoctrinated—or perhaps all three simultaneously. In order for you to do that, I have to tell you flat out: I'm the CEO and founder of PayActiv. That, dear readers, is a company that is making a business out of enabling employers of all sizes to do more for many of their lesser-paid staff.

That is, PayActiv enables businesses large and small to set up a system in which the employee has access to their earnings when they need the money, without having to wait for payday to come along. Given that 90 million people in America live paycheck to paycheck, it is but common sense to let workers access what belongs to them.

Why is this so important? Well, it's a core subtext through this writing: providing a deeper understanding and appreciation for the gap between living life as a relative *have* and experiencing subsistence as a relative *have-not*.

And please let me assure you of this: I am by no means some flaming socialist. At least I don't believe I am. Can a Silicon Valley entrepreneur be a socialist? Frankly, I see myself more as a devotee of pragmatism, social justice, and fairness. By drawing upon all I have seen in life, global demographics, and economics, I worry about growing income disparity. For example, in works like French economist Thomas Piketty's *Capital in the Twenty-First Century*, I detect the seeds of the next event along the lines of the Russian or French revolutions. Nothing imminent, but arising. And rather than fuel the fire, I believe there are many practical things we can do as pragmatists and capitalists that will lessen the plight of our fellow workers while also improving our own bottom lines.

> 90 million people in America live paycheck to paycheck.

2

Click Here for "About"

Visit any website, and the coding will highlight the company's products and more than likely help drive site visitors to deeper engagement and ideally a purchase. But if you want further background, it's always useful to go to the very bottom of the landing page to click "about."

"About" is where you find information *about* the corporate structure, background of the business, maybe some case studies, blogs, and short articles emphasizing the company's commitment to customer satisfaction, cultural diversity, and saving the rainforests. It's also where you'll find staff biographies, and—warning—I'm about to bore you with my own.

I say bore. It's boring to me because I've lived it. It's also intensively uncomfortable. I am not one to prattle on about my own accomplishments or the lack thereof.

So, why tell you at all? I'm trusting those around me: those with whom I work; those who invest in my businesses, past and present; many of my customers; many of my family and friends. Their counsel to me is this: yours, Safwan, is not the typical corporate biography. You've led a diverse and complicated life, and unquestionably your experiences color your perceptions and observations.

Still, to be frank, even when pressed on such issues, so many of the details of my earlier years I've already forgotten. I suspect it's the same for nearly all of us—that, instead of looking back, we are looking to the future.

Nonetheless, it is in the interests of truly full disclosure, along with the insistence from others close to me, that stories, vignettes, and rants to come later will be enriched by greater perspective on the author himself in advance.

Safwan Shah: The Hollywood Years

I'll say it was my homage to Quentin Tarantino, telling this story using no immediately discernable timeline. But, in truth, it's just the nature of my recall.

The first major film project I was to work on featured a no better known nor harder working lead talent than Tom Hanks—along with a similarly noteworthy director, Ron Howard. In prepping for his role of Commander Jim Lovell in this 1995 film epic, *Apollo 13*, Tom needed greater insight into what it means to be completely weightless. Enter the Vomit Comet or what we knew affectionately as the Vomitron—the latter not to be confused with the heavy metal band of the same name.

You are probably aware that NASA uses large transport aircraft fitted with special padding to familiarize would-be astronauts with zero gravity. The plane, a modified KC-135 jet transport, flies in a series of parabolic arcs, generating a period of "freefall" during the twenty-five seconds or so that it drops from peak to trough.

What you might not realize is that this brief zero-gravity joy ride is followed by a 2G transition into a new climb, a new peak, and another freefall—a process that may be repeated as many as fifty or more times on each training flight.

Note that a key challenge in a no- or limited-gravity environment is to learn how to stay calm and focused in order to be able to carry out the most basic activities: like moving, sleeping, or going to the bathroom. Take eating, for instance: what makes food go down the esophagus to the stomach? Gravity, that's what. And when there is no gravity, things can get rather uncomfortable. Time spent in space, they tell me, results in an almost endless feeling of nausea. A key purpose of enduring the Vomitron is to train yourself in how to conquer this feeling and keep everything down. Indeed, fifty cycles from trough to peak and back again gives a whole new meaning to the expression "ad nauseam."

So, where were we? Oh yes, my experiment. As fate would have it, the flight that included my experimental setup for zero-g (absence of gravity that leads to weightlessness) included a very famous passenger named Tom Hanks. Being a perfectionist, he was there to train for *Apollo 13* to appear as realistic as possible in the film. Now I would have liked to have been included on that KC-135 myself—it definitely sounds like fun, doesn't it? But, as it turns out, as a foreign national I wasn't cleared for such adventures. Instead, my lab colleagues had to arrange for someone who was in the flight and looking for a complete experience to flip the various switches to initiate, manage, and complete the experiment.

Fast-forward a week, where I waited anxiously to get my hands on the collected data, and I eventually did, except it had a bad smell. What else did you expect from the ever-so-reliable Vomitron? Except, in this situation, the big story told to me was that my experimental module had been the recipient of Tom Hanks's vomit because he had thrown up in the flight and apparently he had also been tasked to flip the control switches on my experiment. To this day, I can't say with certainty whether or not it was Tom's vomit or just a prank by my colleagues. What I do know is that he won two Best Actor Oscars in the next few years.

> To this day, I can't say with certainty whether or not it was Tom's vomit. What I do know is that he won two best actor Oscars after being in the same flight as my experiment.

I'm in the Wrong Field

By now you've no doubt gleaned that my field was science, not Hollywood. But, more specifically, my background at the time was in electrical engineering. So, the question becomes: What am I doing conducting complex life sciences experiments for a NASA lab and peripherally touching Hollywood actors? A bit more backstory is needed.

While pursuing my electrical engineering undergrad at NED University in Pakistan, I fell in love with a "batchmate" who was in civil engineering. After a four-year courtship, the two of us got married and lived happily, until the vicissitudes of life demanded a change. "Coming to America" was that change, and we decided to pursue graduate studies together at University of Colorado at Boulder. Her goal was to pursue a masters in civil engineering; mine was to achieve a PhD in electrical engineering.

Once in America, however, matters became complicated. I won't go into too much detail here, but suffice to say that, because of a political *fatwa* in Iran and bloody protests in many countries, my wife was forced to go into a sort of hiding here in the US. Where this left us was in a state of physical separation: she moved to Stanford University; I continued in Boulder.

Along the way, no doubt fueled by our forced separation, my wife and I grew more distant but still devoted to each other. Fifteen months later, upon finishing my master's degree, I figured I should give up pursuing a PhD and go back to Pakistan, which I did try for a few months.

Ah, yes, Pakistan, the land of my birth. I was born in Karachi, Pakistan, at Seventh Day Adventist Hospital. My father, an electrical engineer, worked for the government and was regularly transferred to different cities. His explanation for these frequent transfers: he was too honest an officer, so he had to be moved out when illegal electrical connections and graft payments needed to be made. So, in the first twelve years of my education I attended at least seven different schools—more on that later.

Pakistan—Then and Now

Let me next tell you this, Pakistan today is not the same as it was when I was young. In those days, Pakistan hadn't yet become a volatile place as it is now, and most Americans still came there to get the best weed and climb some of the highest mountains in the world. But then came the Iranian revolution. Soon thereafter, Afghanistan became the epicenter of a massive proxy war. On behalf of the US, this neighboring nation became a training ground for various tribes to weaken the communist invaders. Yes, these were the Mujahideen, and this is where the seeds of the Taliban were planted. There are plenty of books on that topic, so I won't dwell on it, but for a clearer perspective, I do recommend you watch Tom Hanks's *Charlie Wilson's War*.

So, yes, my world was changing fast. Start with religion. Today there are religious fanatics in all corners of the world, but when I was a child that just wasn't the case. So, yes, my world was changing fast. Start with religion. Today there are religious fanatics in all corners of the world, but when I was a child that just wasn't the case.

Now my parents are Muslims who migrated to Pakistan from India—and I guess that gives me a default religion, too. But the truth is, I can't be too sure. I spent way too many years in Christian missionary schools. And for that, let me give thanks to my mother. Having grown up in England, she had tremendous command of the English language. Add to this her charm and intelligence, and she was able to convince the nuns that, yes, her son was a perfect match for their all girl's school, Sacred Heart. No, there was no deception at play and, no, I was not required to attend in a frock. It's just that I had an older sister, age six, already in attendance, and with convincing from my mother, the school agreed it would be okay for her four-year-old brother to come along.

After Sacred Heart, I transferred to St. Mary's in Sukkur. Later, we moved to Quetta, Baluchistan, and there I attended St. Francis Grammar School from fourth through seventh grade. Quetta is probably the highest city in the world, about eight thousand feet above sea level and right next to Iran.

These days Quetta is the scene of lot of violence. But even back then, just about everyone in attendance at this school was the son of a tribal chief or leader; all would move in gangs and carry guns wherever they went.

Though by no means effeminate, neither was I the aggressive, dominant sort. Needless to say, I was feeling powerless in this atmosphere, limited in my span of control. When reflecting on that time period even today, I can envision myself shrinking down to the size of a toy action figure among these powerful, full-grown men.

Later, when I was in eighth grade, we moved to Hyderabad where I was able to attend St. Bonaventure School. And it was here that my love of the written word took hold. Father Todd, the principal, was an incredible person who taught us English and poetry. Though he could be strict—reprimanding us with a small stick when needed—he also opened my eyes to new ideas and new, more critical but also compassionate ways of thinking.

Father Todd was remarkably positive and influential, but, as for my love of reading, he was merely building on an already solid foundation. For me, reading had always been a means of escape. Growing up, our house was always full of books, and I read all I could. My parents quoted Shakespeare. I was reading classics like *20,000 Leagues Under the Sea*, *Les Miserables*, *The Count of Monte Cristo*, and even Louis L'Amour westerns.

Reading, I became Captain Nemo, a gunslinger, Edmond Dantès, or other heroes—all active/masculine stuff. But it was at St. Bonaventure, with inspiration from Father Todd, that my interests expanded to softer poetry, including the likes of Alexander Pope and William Wordsworth.

That all said, please let me assure you: I wasn't just a bookworm. In addition, I was incredibly fond of cricket, tennis, and badminton, and was good enough to play on my schools' teams in multiple sports. Today? I'm an avid golfer, playing at almost every opportunity.

Something Wicked

There are two Pakistans in my experience. Pakistan today is not the place I once knew. When I was young, the men in the streets had no religious beards, and on almost any evening in town you could see people frequenting restaurants, bars, and nightclubs. Music was all around; it was a free and colorful time.

But there had been a coup in 1977 by a general who was building an ever-closer relationship with the US. You see, there were evil communists in Afghanistan, and it was vital for the US to finance just about any group that could counter this red threat. Back to my Hollywood roots: do you recall watching *Rambo III*? Filmed in 1988, its Afghanistan-themed plot could have been set just down the road from my home.

So, suddenly, the entire nation transformed from democracy to dictatorship; from relatively secular to Muslim/authoritarian. Groups that had once been in the minority—in the background and unable to assert their authority—were now taking control. Religious groups made the most fanatical and effective fighters, and so they received the lion's share of US largesse.

Things changed noticeably for the worse in the early 1980s. And the changes to my nation were changing me. I became even more secular, almost radical in my thinking. Pakistan was fast becoming a war zone, fighting a needless war, and I grew increasingly angry watching the country move from progressive to religious, even getting myself involved in active protests before realizing that the rot was unstoppable. There were far too many dangers in protesting, so I also embraced mediocrity and ignored the elephant in our midst before getting married and then heading off to the United States of America.

It was after completing my masters in electrical engineering that I returned to Pakistan from Boulder to join my uncle's electronics business. Militarization of the region meant that his company was now supplying the Pakistani military with radios, transceivers, and similarly high-demand equipment.

Not everything we made was defense related, however. For example, I managed his production line that assembled panels and various components into a product we called *FirstWatch*—one of the first solar-powered alarm/security systems available for your RV! Every month, we shipped a few thousand *FirstWatch* units to RadioShack to warn campers that an intruder—I always imagined a bear—was nearby.

> Suddenly, the entire nation transformed from democracy to dictatorship; from relatively secular to Muslim/authoritarian.

I could prosper in Pakistan. But having been in the US for fifteen months, I found the contrast between a free and a not-so-free society painfully evident, and soon found myself thinking: there is no place for me in this now cold, warlike, and decidedly corrupt place. And so I wrote a letter to my professor at Boulder asking if I could return, and he answered affirmatively. I recall the plane ride back to America; I was delighted to be returning "home."

Where's the Funding?

Electrical engineering had been my focus. But UC Boulder is a hotbed of NASA-financed activity. And so I switched over to the world of aerospace engineering as a way to get my tuition funded by my PhD advisor/sponsor, Marvin Luttges. "Marv" had founded BioServe Space Technologies, a research center inside Boulder's Aerospace Engineering Department, and it is here that I got a chance to use my background in electrical engineering to design experiments that over time ended up as part of various space shuttle missions.

Outside Marv's office there was a poster: "The meek shall inherit the Earth; the rest of us are going to the stars." Well, one of the things we realized was that, en route to Mars or elsewhere, we're going to be living in decidedly different conditions. And so I developed a means of investigation, of creativity. The idea is simple: think about what changes are expected in general, and then think of what that might mean for life and living, specifically.

First of all, as Tom Hanks was learning, in space there will be a lot of zero-gravity situations—that is, unless we find ways to compensate, such as the spinning sections of space vessels we saw in *2001: A Space Odyssey* or more recently in *Martian* or *Passengers*. Still, a key research question becomes: What happens to the human body in microgravity? Or my favorite: how do you grow plants in space? If there is limited gravity during a space voyage or when living on a new world, how will plants grow? Specifically, will roots and shoots know which direction to grow in order to function and survive? Or how will we get the water to the soil and root system?

One of my experiments designed to answer this question made it on board three different experimental zero-g missions—in part, thanks to the successful prototype whose switch got flipped by Tom Hanks. Essentially, I created a series of analog sensors whose signals could later be combined to 3D/digitally illustrate how water would flow in microgravity. How much water, for example, could be drawn to a seed or plant by capillary action alone? The only way to find out is to run a zero-g test. And such early experiments, I humbly insist, helped contribute to the learning that today enables hydroponic plant growth on board the International Space Station.

It was also our work that figured out a substitute for soil. To grow a great tomato, or any other fruit or vegetable (some are still surprised to learn that the tomato is a fruit!), you need a substrate to hold the nutrients and water as well as anchor the seed and root system. On Earth? We use dirt. Okay, my botanist friends immediately will correct that and say "soil." But in space travel, we are always looking to conserve and optimize weight. And whether you call it dirt or soil, it's relatively heavy. So, one of the useful things we learned at UC Boulder? Rockwool, already prized for being a flame-retardant insulator, is also a lightweight and effective substrate. Bury a seed in that upstairs insulation, throw in some nutrients and water, and things will grow—even in space.

Apogee . . .

Other experiments and research at UC Boulder were less interstellar. Like how to ensure that Coca-Cola kept its fizz in space, or how to mix liquids so that the suspension was perfect. And then there was the project that would eventually help me to earn my PhD: an analysis of interneuronal communication in the thoracic ganglia of the cricket (stay tuned).

The height of my experience in Boulder—the apogee of this chapter in my life—was my time working with BioServe, a NASA center for the commercialization of space. Yeah, you read it right—commercialization of space. In broad terms, it meant thinking and building around those ideas that would make it possible for humanity to survive in space. Perhaps it was there and then that the seeds of transporting people into space were planted and a young Elon Musk or Jeff Bezos were inspired to launch SpaceX and Blue Origin. But it was more than that: in my lab, various astronauts would come and go, often arriving in jets they piloted themselves. These astronauts were like John Wayne, Rocky, and George Washington all rolled into one. They were amazing people, on the cutting edge of human achievement, and it was my profound privilege to contribute some infinitesimal scientific knowledge to that sacred journey.

. . . and Perigee—My Brush with Financial Despair a.k.a. Poverty

As for the perigee, the lowest point, I'd have to say it began when my wife had to move away from me due to those aforementioned political circumstances. Living apart can strain or break almost any relationship. We tried, but could not succeed. It was a failure, and it weighed on me, whether clear to others or not.

Our parting was not only emotionally painful, however; it soon became economically excruciating as well, providing me with an eye-opening brush with financial despair, and the stresses one encounters when living a life of continuous, unrelenting financial duress.

At work in the lab one morning—I had been working around the clock—a colleague informed me there had been a call, someone needing to speak with me about a personal issue.

I was devastated. I felt hopeless. My honor had been eviscerated, and after only a short time, the issue was quite visibly impacting my work.

As it turned out, unbeknownst to me, I was being saddled with an American Express Card debt that had moved into collection. No, it hadn't been my account. No, I hadn't seen any of the prior notices. But, as I've since learned, this is the sort of thing that often happens in divorces.

So, there I was, barely scraping by on a meager stipend of an academic researcher while pursuing a PhD—all of $1,150 a month. And while I had been carrying some minor credit card debt already, without my knowledge the total had swelled to $30,000, two-thirds of which was immediately due and payable. How would I pay this loan? My honor had been eviscerated, and after only a short time, the issue was quite visibly impacting my work.

Soon enough, Professor Luttges took it upon himself to talk with me about the situation. After I shared how deeply this was diminishing my spirit and sense of self-worth, instead of offering some sort of Solomon-like revelation, he simply laughed. And I do mean gut laughter.

He said to me: This is America. This is where intelligent, highly-educated, and successful people screw up financially, declare bankruptcy or whatever, and then move on with their lives. This happens frequently, I was told, and so it's nothing to be ashamed of. Rather, he explained, it was time for bootstrapping.

He said I should call a consumer credit counseling service. They helped me to take inventory of all of my income and expenses, and soon determined that my monthly, consolidated debt payment would total $750 a month, which amounted to leaving just $400 from my monthly stipend of $1,150 to pay all my other expenses. They tore up my credit cards, and I donned a $400-a-month financial straitjacket.

So, it was during this period that I learned what it's like to be truly cash-strapped and poor. Living paycheck to paycheck and without any credit or savings was an incredibly stressful experience. More accurately, it was like an abusive relationship. Every time I got hit by another late, overdraft, or NSF (non-sufficient funds) fee, I actually felt that I deserved it.

Living on so little per month was quite hard. Every few days or so I got into a situation where I needed a small amount like $20, and I simply didn't have it. I recall a time when for days on end the only meal I ate was an omelet. Eggs are cheap and high in nutrition.

Scrimping, getting by with only the essentials—this was something I could do for a time. But I also realized that at some point the debt would be paid and the suffering could end. Moreover, with my credentials, I would be able to get a higher paying position. And, in fact, owing this debt and wanting to pay it back quickly led to my decision to move to Silicon Valley, and eventually to settle in the US.

Perhaps, it is why I became an entrepreneur, too. I knew I was a survivor; after all, I had already seen my bottom—and survived. I was the lucky one. I had help from my professor, I didn't have children during that time, and I was highly educated. Now I was also fearless, ready to take on any challenge.

◼ IN PRACTICE

- We learn the most from downward spirals (that is *IF* we survive or are allowed to survive).
- There is always help around the corner; don't give up.
- Financial adversity can happen to anyone, but the question becomes: What can you do in your business to help lessen its side effects?

In a world going real-time, the batch payroll process is a twisted way to treat employees.

SAFWAN SHAH

Chapter Two

Life's a Batch

A brief, enlightening, and somewhat surprising look at the history of employee payment processes

- *What is a batch?*
- *Payment practices in "ancient" times*
- *Colonial payment woes: indentured servitude*
- *The notorious "company store"*
- *How the IRS institutionalized batch payments*
- *Religion, science, and technology agree: the batch must go!*

■ ■ ■

Whether you realize this or not, much of your life takes place in batch mode. Telegraphing where we're going with this chapter and this book, I will tell you my opinion on such matters:

We need to kill the batch.

Defining the Batch

A batch is any process placed on hold while individual transactions or events accumulate until, finally, matters are ready for simultaneous processing. All the loaves of bread go through the oven at one time; all of the evening's bar tabs are uploaded to a central processor awaiting the next run. We can't have what we want right now. We can't do what we want right now. Even if we want just a single loaf of freshly baked bread, we still have to wait for the batch to complete.

Among my first truly conscious experiences was in the computer sciences lab, during just one of those courses needed to obtain a degree in engineering. There we were studying programming, Fortran IV, and we would write our programs, then transfer the instructions into that stack of punch cards. All of the students would hand in their stacks. But instead of the instantaneous processing we've come to expect from our laptops, back then we had to wait until late that afternoon or evening when all of the various students' programs were batch-fed into the mainframe.

Waiting for the results of a program, all that queuing, was excruciating enough. But the truly frustrating thing was that, if for some reason there was some little item in a program that wasn't quite right, if the precise holes were not punched, or a minor command was mistyped, out went the entire program. It just wouldn't run. Want to fail at computers? Wait until the last minute to submit your program, when batch processing will prevent you from having time to review and repair your work.

But the batch system wasn't invented by computer scientists. Just think about media. Growing up in the '70s and '80s, everything was appointment television. That is, if you weren't in front of the screen when the latest episode of (name your favorite series or sitcom) or the Super Bowl or Cricket World Cup or the Emmy Awards was airing, you missed it. Best case? For certain series, you could wait three to six months, and the program would repeat. It wasn't until the late 1970s that VCRs reached a price point accessible to anyone other than a television studio, and, by the early '80s, recording televised programs became common.

With the introduction of a VCR affordable to the masses, media moved away from batch-oriented delivery and toward on-demand delivery—although, most veterans of the period can still remember the flashing light syndrome and how difficult it was to actually get the VCR to record the right program at the right time. And, of course, today, nearly all programming is on demand.

"Bankers' hours," a common term since its first use in the 1800s, refers to the fact that banks used to be open for business only on weekdays between ten a.m. and four p.m., primarily so there would be enough time left in the afternoon to process all the transactions received that day. Checks had to be debited and deposits credited to accounts whose balances were then recomputed, with everything made ready for the next day's batch of transactions.

But, like bankers' hours, today the batch is disappearing wherever we look. Shopping? Prior to the late 1970s, most stores were closed on Sundays. Moreover, almost no businesses whatsoever—not even gas stations or restaurants—opened their doors on major US holidays like Christmas, Thanksgiving, or Easter. If you wanted to "go out" for a dinner in those days, you had to choose whether to eat at a hotel or at a Chinese or Indian restaurant.

And today? We no longer need to wait for anything. Spending has been made almost frictionless. Just about anything a person could want can be ordered 24-7 via an online system. Amazon Prime is already offering same-day service in many ZIP codes. As demand grows and logistics processes become more efficient (and supported by drones), in a few years we may all expect online orders to be delivered to us within the hour.

We no longer need to wait for anything.

But now think about your paycheck, when you get paid your earnings in weekly, biweekly, or even monthly batches. Millennials may find this difficult to believe: a mere twenty years ago, the vast majority of employees were still receiving their pay in the form of a slip of paper. On a Thursday or Friday afternoon, the mail cart would stop by each worker's desk to drop off an envelope, inside of which was a batch-produced payment instruction form known as a check. Each check was in turn encoded with the payor's account information in magnetic ink, the amount to pay each worker, and either a hand- (common for small companies) or machine-generated signature of the appropriate corporate officer for authorizing the transfer.

Employees would then have to rush out of the office during their lunch hour to stand in line at a bank to cash their paycheck. When cashed at the bank whose check it was, a bank employee known as a teller would verify the identity of the payee (the employee), verify the signature on the check, then hand over its cash equivalent. If cashed at some bank other than that upon which the check was drawn, clearing the funds and making them available for the employee's use could take another day or two (with the processing performed in batch mode, one day's batch at a time).

> Never seen a check before? Spend an afternoon at a local supermarket and pay close attention.

Never seen a check before? Spend an afternoon at a local supermarket and pay close attention. Sooner or later a customer will pull a slim rectangular wallet from their purse or pocket, ask the clerk for a pen, and then take several minutes completing one of these requests for an overnight payment to the store—via batch processing, of course.

The Ancient Promise of Pay in Batches

How long have workers been enslaved by the tyranny of batch payroll? The history of money teaches us that for many centuries there were no truly flexible mechanisms for exchanging one person's labor for something of comparable value. Before the invention of money, there was no easy way to store value or to transfer value in desired increments.

When contemplating trade, circa 350 BCE, Aristotle called barter "a coincidence of wants." That is, before an exchange could take place, enough value would need to accumulate in one object to make it an appropriate swap for another object: this handmade candle for that hand-fired clay pot. Or maybe three or four different objects might contain enough value to swap for a single other object: these clay-fired plates and cups along with these forged-steel cutting tools in exchange for that saddle. So, a deal could not be struck until, via a series of uneven batch processes, the buyer/seller ledgers equilibrated. And this challenge applied to the exchange of labor as well. How long must a worker toil until they're owed which item? If one day's labor is worth a fifth of a goat, then the soonest the worker can expect to be paid is at the end of the fifth day.

But then along came money—and credit—making it easier to store and exchange wealth in flexible quantities, thus facilitating freer, more exacting exchanges. Unfortunately for many in the working class, however, this still didn't mean real-time pay. And as for those in the warrior class—soldiers—pay could be even more elusive.

Generals and kingdoms of old employed batch payments to an almost unconscionable degree. As Alexander the Great conquered country after country, kingdom after kingdom, his need for additional soldiers was nearly insatiable. But how to convince once-conquered enemies to join his ranks? What we can understand from accounts of the time is that he did so with the promise of future pay for today's toils and risks.

> Generals and kingdoms of old employed batch payments to an almost unconscionable degree.

That is, he would feed, clothe, and arm these men for battle, but their real payoff would only come when the final enemy was vanquished, and the lucky soldiers would be free to loot and pillage to their hearts' content.

The same was true for the Mongol Empire of Temujin, a.k.a. Genghis Khan. As they swept from city to city, Khan's warriors understood their payday would arrive if and only if the army was victorious. So, soldier on they would, not partaking of the spoils of war—their pay—until the campaign batch was fully processed.

Indeed, all the great generals of ancient history inspired their followers with dreams of great victories and promises of plunder. It was trickle-down economics in its earliest form. You are given enough to stay alive. But help our great cause to victory, and you will share in the spoils.

Colonial Payment

For most of history, employers set the terms of a laborer's pay, whether in barter or plunder or coinage.

But those who would seek to hire the skills of others have not always had the upper hand in wage negotiations. There was a time in US history, for example, when workers were able to set the terms. Citing various sources, a 1933 bulletin from the US Department of Labor notes the following:

> A colonial treasurer of the Virginia Colony declared, about 1625, that the wages paid there were "intolerable" and "much in excess of the sum paid to the same class of persons in England." In 1633 Governor Winthrop, of the Massachusetts Bay Colony, noted that the "excessive rates" charged by workmen "grew to a general complaint" which called for legislative action, and a colonial governor in North Carolina complained that "the Price of Labour is very high."[1]

Presumably, those who can command relatively high rates of compensation would also be in a strong position to insist on timing of payment. But the ruling class (yes, every society has a "ruling class," even great democracies) was not to be constrained for long. The report goes on to explain,

> Throughout [this] colonial period, scarcity was a vital problem that influenced customs and legislation and resulted in the establishment of the elaborate system of securing workers by contract or "indenture."[2] . . .

---

1   *History of Wages in the United States from Colonial Times to 1928* (Washington, D.C.: US Government Printing Office, 1934), 7.

2   Ibid.

Both of these conditions, the scarcity of labour and the resulting high wages, were met differently by the Northern and the
Southern colonies. Out of them grew the indenture system
and, eventually in the South, slavery.[3]

So, whatever power scarcity granted to any individual trades-
person to control the level and timing of payment, in one way or
another government and society at large found mechanisms to
import scarce skills at a lesser, fixed price. A letter from the director of one of the colonies to their commissioners concludes: "Free
smiths are extraordinarily scarce," and, because of the price they
were in consequence able to command, "it is not advisable to get
much work done by them."[4]

Company Stores and IPOs

It was some thirty years ago that I first observed someone asking
an employer for a salary advance. The request was simple: "It is the
seventeenth of the month. May I please have ten days' pay, and
then you can deduct it on the first when I get paid?" Fair enough,
I thought. After all, this individual had already earned their money.
Yet, the retort from the employer was anything but accommodating.
"No. You need to take control of your life and manage your finances
better. I am not your bank and not a lender."

I was taken aback, and today what I remember most from that
exchange was that someone in need had asked for money—*money
they had already earned*—and had been refused. Rudely, self-
righteously refused.

Today's employment relationship is a form of private contract,
and today's lower-wage employees have acquiesced to accept this
contract, which includes batch payment for labor rendered. The
labor is rendered in real time, but the payment is not. And not only

---

3 Ibid, 8.

4 Ibid.

have employers been able to delay their payrolls, they have also found ways to *charge* workers for the privilege.

Before the age of automobiles, workers were often lured to find employment in industries like mining, lumbering, or railroad construction, where the work required living in some of the most remote areas imaginable at the time. But working so far from civilization, these workers in turn would need all manner of essentials, from milk, butter, and eggs to clothing. Many companies responded to this demand by setting up their own "company store."

Of course, this was a convenience for workers. But it was also a recipe for abuse, since the company store was, nearly by definition, a monopoly. Not all such establishments took advantage of the situation, but it could be relatively easy for workers to wind up paying exorbitant prices for their everyday needs along with becoming indebted—borrowing against their own accruing wages.

> The company store was, nearly by definition, a monopoly.

Growing up in Pakistan, I was surrounded by music. My mother, eclectic in her own tastes, continuously exposed me to a wide range of artists and styles. The song "Sixteen Tons" is one that, for some reason, really stood out and stuck with me. Written and pressed by Merle Travis, but covered in dozens of recordings by diverse artists from Tennessee Ernie Ford to Stevie Wonder, it immortalizes the idea that the company store was simply a mechanism for turning a willing employee into a de facto indentured servant:

> You load sixteen tons, what do you get?
> Another day older and deeper in debt.
> Saint Peter don't you call, because I can't go,
> I owe my soul to the company store.[5]

Fast-forward to today's era of entrepreneurs and go-go startups. Today, it seems that all one needs to be successful is the promise

---

5   Merle Travis, *Sixteen Tons* (BMI, 1946).

that a particular idea, application, technology, or whatever will disrupt all of society and commerce. Still, everyone realizes that it's never the mere idea that wins the day; true success is all about execution, and execution will always require human labor of some type.

So, it takes an evangelist leader to recruit and inspire teams of true believers willing to work for next to nothing, sixty, seventy, eighty hours per week, possibly for years on end, with only the hope—never a promise—that one day soon some angel investor will appear or, better still, an IPO. Like the armies of Genghis Khan and Alexander, the soldiers fight the battles never knowing for certain if or when the spoils will actually materialize.

But even for someone who isn't willing to give up so much of their current human labor for some uncertain future (such as any relatively lower-wage worker), the reality is that their compensation will be doled out *in arrears*. The reality is that employers routinely withhold two weeks' pay (or even more) from each of their workers, simply as a consequence of the batch processing model of operation.

The idea is sold to employees as "it takes time for the information to get to the payroll processor." And this rationale at one time may have held a kernel of truth. But in today's world of instantaneous data flows, this technologically outdated practice does little more than help to ensure that lower-wage workers will continue showing up for their shifts and performing as directed, knowing that the employer holds such leverage.

In point of fact, the employer is now using the employee as a source of credit—and at zero interest, no less.

In point of fact, the employer is now using the employee as a source of credit—and at zero interest, no less. "Another day older and deeper in debt" indeed.

The IRS Transforms Payroll

Recall that the powers that be in the New World collaborated to thrust the migrating masses into indentured servitude, and even outright slavery when necessary, to ensure that the cost of labor remained low. But government hasn't always been the bad guy in the story of global subjugation by batch—oftentimes it has served as a counter.

Human resources (HR) laws and customs of today go a long way toward protecting the rights of workers. Of course, employers will counter that having so many rules actually tends to depress employment. Moreover, local governments that have taken steps such as raising their local or regional minimum wage have seen mixed results at best.

But looking specifically at the history of the *timing* of payroll, it was the US Internal Revenue Service (IRS), in the 1920s, that instituted a seismic shift in the pace of employee payment. Acting out of its own need for greater predictability, rules were written to require corporations to forward their tax payments on a quarterly basis. The batch was mandated by US tax law, and it was to process no less frequently than every three months.

> The batch was mandated by US tax law, and it was to process no less frequently than every three months.

From there, the rules piled on. It came to a point where, for any accumulated tax liability on a payroll that exceeded $100,000, the IRS required a tax payment that same week. Then, wanting their share of payroll taxes as well, various states began writing their own laws requiring more frequent payments. It was likely an unintended set of consequences, but as government demanded a stricter payment schedule and batch systems were so calibrated, workers also began to receive wages in a more deterministic manner. A small victory, perhaps, but a victory nonetheless.

Religion, Science, and Technology Agree?

It isn't all that often that religion, science, and technology arrive at the same conclusion. But when it comes to batched payroll, the vote is unanimous: the batch must go.

It's no secret that the lowest paid among us must always plan more carefully to avoid random financial disasters, so they are much more cognizant of exactly how much they will be paid, and when. Ask the typical, relatively high-wage salaried office professional how much they've earned "today," and you'll likely see a shrug of the shoulders—what, me worry? But ask this of a scheduled hourly worker like a call-center operator, or a fast-food worker, or (to take this to the extreme) of an illegal immigrant day worker who gets paid in cash, and you'll discover that those at the lowest ends of the pay spectrum have a much clearer idea of what their labors can buy for them—by the hour, by the day, and by the week. When you have no margin for error, you can't afford the luxury of *not* knowing. Because, when you are poor, as Moses once said, you are *counting* on the pay you'll be receiving.

Deuteronomy 24:15, purported to be the words of the prophet Moses culled from a series of three sermons delivered on the plains of Moab, puts it this way:

> Do not take advantage of a hired worker who is poor and needy, whether that worker is a fellow Israelite or a foreigner residing in one of your towns.
>
> Pay them their wages each day before sunset, because they are poor and are counting on it. Otherwise they may cry to the lord against you, and you will be guilty of sin.[6]

In fact, all of the Abrahamic faiths—Christianity, Islam, Judaism—have something to say about when workers should be paid. Proverbs 3:28, also found in both the Torah and the Old Testament, puts it even more succinctly, directing the following:

---

6   Deut. 24:15 (New International Version), https://www.biblegateway.com/passage/?search=Deuteronomy+24%3A15&version=NIV.

Do not say to your neighbor, "Come back tomorrow and I'll give it to you"—when you already have it with you.[7]

In Islam, there is a Hadith (words of the prophet): pay the laborer his wages before his sweat dries.[8]

The religious tradition is clear: Paying your workers what they are owed in a *timely* way is a fundamental moral responsibility. But what does science have to say on the subject?

George Akerlof is the winner of the 2001 Nobel Prize[9] in economic sciences as well as husband to former Fed Chairperson Janet Yellen. Robert Shiller won his Nobel in 2013 and is also known for publishing the Case-Shiller housing index (proving year in and year out that housing prices over time do not truly rise). Shiller is widely held to have predicted both the tech bubble in 2001 and the housing bubble in 2008.

Collaborating to write the 2015 book *Phishing for Phools: The Economics of Manipulation and Deception*,[10] Akerlof and Shiller argue that businesses, including employers, will do whatever it takes to extract greater profits for themselves, with little regard for whatever damage their effort might do to others. It is their nature. In particular, "Competitive markets by their very nature spawn deception and trickery; [there is a] a phishing equilibrium in which every chance for profit more than the ordinary will be taken up."

Their book is replete with examples of how businesses routinely deceive the masses to extract excess returns. Advertising makes us buy what we don't need. Widely available credit makes us spend what we don't have. Drugs we're taking don't deliver the purported effect.

Certainly, the profit motive and capitalism have delivered the world greater wealth and health than has ever been known in

7   Prov. 3:28 (New International Version), https://www.biblegateway.com/passage/?search=Proverbs+3%3A28&version=NIV.

8   "Pay the Laborer his Wages Before his Sweat Dries," Mercy to Mankind, February 27, 2018, http://www.masjidma.com/2018/02/27/the-employer-employee-relationship/.

9   Shared with Michael Spence and Joseph E. Stiglitz.

10 George A. Akerlof and Robert J. Shiller, *Phishing for Phools: The Economics of Manipulation and Deception* (Princeton: Princeton University Press, 2015).

history. And many employers have learned that human nature itself dictates that when workers are paid more often—when there is a closer correlation between the goal and the reward—they will be more task-focused and productive for the employer.

On the other hand, when profit is pursued with no regard to anything else (which seems to happen more and more frequently), it can lead to terrible suffering. Consider what happens time and again around the world during periods of drought or famine, for instance.

People usually don't die in such instances because of any real lack of food and water—the provisions are there. Instead, they die because of distribution systems that get clogged by earnest, church-going capitalists simply holding back for higher profits. Even if the warehouses are full, the commodity owners know keenly well that, with each day of further delay, prices will rise and profits will rise still higher. There is always money to be made by using the batch as a tool for exacerbating a shortage. Kill the batch.

There is always money to be made by using the batch as a tool for exacerbating a shortage. Kill the batch.

Want more science? In *The Timing of Pay*, researchers Christopher Parsons and Edward Van Wesep use sophisticated mathematics crossed with behavioral science to evaluate the optimum pay periods across the full spectrum of wage levels. One of their key conclusions, based on this analysis, is that "[w]orkers who make less—and therefore have less of a savings buffer with which to smooth consumption—should be paid more frequently."[11] This is a scientific finding, but one can almost hear Moses's voice: "Pay them their wages each day before sunset, because they are poor and are counting on it."

Science and religion both support ending the batch process with respect to payroll, not just because it is inefficient, but because it is unjust as well.

---

11 Christopher Parsons and E. Van Wesep, *The Timing of Pay* (The Society of Labor Economists, 2011), p. 2, https://www.sole-jole.org/12082.pdf.

And technology? Technology tells us that, when decisions are not being made in real time, fully loaded with all the information available, then the system is not intelligent. Intelligent systems execute their tasks when they are needed. In concert. On demand.

Batch processing represents nothing less than a pointless and wasteful form of extremely unsynchronized action. Batch processing adds weeks of unnecessary "latency" to a system that, with today's tools, could easily be operated in real time.

Kill the Batch-Process Payday Before It Kills You

Batch processing and systems are an artifact of the past. There was a time when batch processing could be a means of achieving efficiency, given the high costs of running a mainframe or the cost/effort of running a production line. In essence, batch systems are borne of the cost/performance ratios that the technology of the time permitted. So, we used batches to align and optimize.

Modern, connected technology, however, has made it easier to distribute, compute, command, communicate, and control. Orchestrating and organizing are much easier. Today we see modern businesses like Amazon, Google, and Netflix finding success by killing a wide range of notable batch processes. In fact, I submit that, whenever we say something in our lives has "gone digital," it often means nothing more than the batch was killed.

It ought to be clear by now that, given today's increasingly capable technologies, batch processing creates many more problems than it solves. But think about a low-wage worker living essentially at a subsistence level. These workers have to wait—two weeks—before they are paid. There is a high cost of waiting to be paid—toxic financial stress. In fact, while waiting to be paid, they often feel forced into making bad decisions like taking out payday loans or missing a payment, which then leads to a hefty late fee. Hence, it should be no surprise that when it is finally payday they binge, leading to the need for even

Yes, the batch is actually killing workers.

more short-term loans. Should a crisis develop—like their car breaks down or they need a doctor—the financial strain intensifies and damages them even more. A vicious cycle indeed.

Even beyond this kind of stress, you may be surprised to learn that batch processing is also *deadly*. Yes, the batch is actually killing workers. The *Economist* reports that workers have a "23% increase in the chance of dying on paydays."[12] Looking at data for public-sector workers over a six-year period, a group of Swedish researchers found that on paydays there were significant increases in "heart problems (a 70% rise in mortality) and strokes (a 120% rise)," primarily "in workers who earned less than average and mostly among the young."[13] The researchers go on to suggest that increased spending on food and leisure activities to reduce stress—take-out meals, trips to football matches, and the like—caused a sudden spike in activity, which led to increased stress and extra deaths.

So why are we still living our lives in batch mode? The reality is, we don't need to.

Nothing good comes from the batch. Scientists don't like it. God doesn't approve of it. Even the IRS has come to disdain the batch payroll. And, as you can likely surmise, I certainly despise the batch, particularly when this vestige of an earlier time inflicts harm—for no good reason whatsoever—on the most fragile among us. For example, I often wonder just how much more easily the lowest-paid workers could understand and manage their financial lives if they could receive their wages when they needed them; in a timely fashion; visibly; freed from the batch.

Data and information today flow instantaneously. Look at services like Airbnb, Uber, or Netflix. Instead of homes lying empty and cities building an excess of hotel rooms; instead of cars sitting parked and taking up precious city space; instead of using tapes or

---

12 "Paydays and Mortality: Cash to Crash," *The Economist*, November 20, 2014, https://www.economist.com/international/2014/11/20/cash-to-crash. Based on the study in Elvira Andersson, Petter Lundborg, and Johan Vikström, "Income Receipt and Mortality—Evidence from Swedish Public-sector Employees," *Journal of Public Economics* 131 (November 2015): 21–32.

13 Ibid.

metal disks to ship video images around: in domain after domain, information technology has replaced highly inefficient batch processes with real-time, on-demand processes, delivering enormous benefits for society.

The batch was once ubiquitous, and now it is nearly extinct. Nearly, but not totally. No, the batch lives on in the antiquated, payroll processes of the modern employer.

It's time to eradicate that quaint vestige of serfdom, conquest, and indentured servitude.

Ding dong, the batch is dead.

Long live real time!

■ IN PRACTICE

- What are your company's payment practices?
- In what ways are they helping your business?
- In what ways might they be harming employees?

Having enjoyed freedom from financial stress, my dream is to help others enjoy that same liberation.

SAFWAN SHAH

> **"**
> *When there is no room for error,*
> *the future can look precipitous and foreboding.*
>
> SAFWAN SHAH

Chapter Three

We Err with Greater Consistency

Day-to-day life is fraught with more mistakes than we realize or typically admit—even to ourselves

- *Golf—and assorted other humiliations*
- *Who are you?—business often gets that wrong*
- *We don't know what we don't know: understanding commitment bias*
- *We all make mistakes—but mistakes thrust disproportionate harm on the poor*
- *Enter the predator: a slew of financial services positioned to "help" the poor amid crises tend to do more harm than good*

■ ■ ■

We all err with greater consistency than we succeed. During our time here on Earth, there are just so many more ways to foul things up than there are paths to a desired accomplishment, utility, or perfection.

The Physics of Sport, Music, and Life

Perhaps nowhere is this more obvious than when playing golf, as any newbie learns early on in their indoctrination to the game. It's on that first tee under the critical gaze of so many friends—to say nothing of the onlookers from the carts and the foursomes awaiting their turns behind—that the nerves tense.

The realization is inescapable. There are just so many ways to humiliate oneself by hideously, pathetically mishitting the golf ball. Such anguish is rational, particularly in relation to the comparatively few paths available for the human body to guide the shaft and club head through space with sufficient pace and accuracy in order to launch any sort of credible shot.

The same is true for football (for American readers, soccer). The margin of error between a well-struck ball that slices through to the net and a flailing quail of a shot that drifts harmlessly wide can be a mere few millimeters (again for Americans, give it an inch) left, right, up or down on the boot (Americans: cleat).

And it's true for learning to play live music—attempting to cover U2, The Beatles, or Bach, it's far easier to sound "okay" than to deliver a truly curtain-calling performance. It's true for theater, dance, driving your car, or learning to garden—almost any human endeavor. The avenues leading to less than perfection are far more numerous than those leading to success.

> The avenues leading to less than perfection are far more numerous than those leading to success.

Certainly, through practice—those ten thousand hours that Malcolm Gladwell suggests are necessary to the mastery of any task—we can reduce the margins of error and gain greater confidence if not the appearance of effortlessness. But the road from the chaos of what might happen to the road of near certainty is, for most activities, a long one.

Where Else Are We Wrong—Which "You" Are We Targeting?

Here is my fear, my dire look at humankind.

The sell side of the world uses our tendency to make errors in order to break down our resistance. We are exploited and manipulated as information about our imperfections allows everyone around us to try and take advantage. They want to manipulate us, to extract greater value from us.

Behavioral and data scientists are hard at work trying to figure out who each one of us is so that we can be more easily targeted by advertising and other related sales efforts. When we walk into a retail store, the owner or salesperson is sizing us up. What kind of car do you drive—and what would you like to drive? What kind of clothes do you wear—and what can we do to drive that next impulse purchase?

Indeed, the predictive power of data can be remarkable. Most are aware of the story of Target—a group whose technology in 2012 could recognize when a couple was likely to have children even before the couple themselves might be aware.[14] But, in fact, such insights date back to the early days of loyalty cards.

An analyst I know well and trust tells me that the UK's Tesco became similarly aware of their ability to understand consumers better than those consumers could understand themselves as early as 2002. Back then, Tesco was publishing quarterly "award points" catalogs customized thousands of ways based on a given house-hold's actual purchases. That is, the cover on the issue sent to the household of a pensioner would be completely different from that of some young cohabitating couple—as would the array of copy/ offers inside. The accuracy, the analyst recalls, was uncanny.

Target, Tesco—and today just about every other major retailer you can think of—now uses tools such as machine learning to comb through data collected from loyalty cards, app usage, website visits, and location video to improve the design and layout of its stores. For instance, retailers use what they know of customer's prefer-ences and tendencies in order to place the highest margin items in precisely the right places to maximize visibility and sales. The bread is in the center of the market, which means that, to get our basic inexpensive commodities, we all have to tread the gauntlet

---

14 Kashmir Hill, "How Target Figured Out a Teen Girl Was Pregnant Before Her Father Did," *Forbes*, February 16, 2012, https://www.forbes.com/sites /kashmirhill/2012/02/16/how-target-figured-out-a-teen-girl-was-pregnant -before-her-father-did/#31cb27626668.

of the processed, higher-margin, salty/sugary, hunger- and thirst-inducing wares.

But let's look even more closely. Target, Tesco, and probably others knew you were having a baby—and so they optimized their offers to you personally, to get you to fill up the most margin-worthy basket. They also knew when your son or daughter began playing soccer, volleyball, or basketball (and the right energy boosters to pitch); when they would be going off to college (need dorm snacks along with study supplies?); and when you started needing dentures. So, for a seller, data can help get things right.

But how often are they wrong? Is it possible to size up everyone's needs, wants, and desires by looks alone? By association? Do we always have the correct data?

After their battery dies, suppose someone were to borrow your smartphone—maybe your wife or son—to do a quick web search for an item. Suddenly your phone and laptop will be pitching you tween video game titles or Elizabethan couture (your spouse loves Renaissance festivals). Oops, the algorithm is erring.

Or perhaps at home, on your laptop, you research a few items for your upcoming camping trip but then head to the sporting goods store to touch,

> Oops, the algorithm is erring.

feel, and evaluate the wares via analog. You wind up buying what you need at the retailer, loading it in your car, and then setting it up on your suburban lawn (or, for urbanites, the dining room floor).

But for the next six weeks, know this: every website you visit, every search you execute will also inundate you with offers for these items that you now already own. The ether (think Amazon) "knows" your past self; it just hasn't caught up with the new you, the proud owner of that tent, camping knife, inflatable canoe, and ax, or whatever else you felt you had to have on this last shopping spree.

You are the victim of dated data—data that describes the you of six weeks ago, but not the you of today. The algorithm is again erring.

We Don't Know What We Don't Know

So how does it feel to make an error? It usually feels like not making an error, that's what. "After all," says author Kathryn Schulz in *Being Wrong: Adventures in the Margin of Error*, "if we knew we were making an error, it wouldn't be an error, would it?"[15]

In his writings on Socrates, Plato developed a concept today known as one of the most crucial Socratic paradoxes: "I know one thing; that I know nothing." Such is the nature of error. By definition, we don't know when we're making errors.

However, if we know something has a high probability of producing an error, we have the option of doing what we can to avoid the mistake. The guitarist can practice. The basketball player can shoot three hundred free throws. The marketer can refine the algorithm and better allocate ad-rendering dollars. (The would-be golfer's best choice might be to instead take up ballroom dancing.)

How does making an error feel? Colossal errors are everywhere—even among the well-rehearsed. Dustin Johnson, faced with a four-foot eagle putt to win the 2015 US Open, misses wide and long. Now, putting just two feet for a push, it appears he hurries, anxious to get through the stress of the competition perhaps, and he misses again. It is a stunning collapse; the pain must be searing; but it reminds us that errors abound in our cosmos.

> Colossal errors are everywhere—even among the well-rehearsed.

Often, we don't know we're making an error. How could we? Until events have run their course, until the passage of time, there is often no means of knowing the path we're on. Moreover, there will be errors we make that we never perceive. For example, how does any child come to recognize that it is a mistake to watch so much television or play so many video games rather than doing homework or reading a book? Wealthier homes have more insight and resources to correct such errors; poorer families may recognize the error but lack the means of effective correction.

---

15 Kathryn Schulz, *Being Wrong: Adventures in the Margin of Error* (Ecco/Harper Collins, 2011), 243.

Or when it begins to seem as though we may have made an error, oftentimes a commitment bias ensues. Instead of correcting the error, we decide to double down. We picked that stock. It's a dog today, but we know in our hearts that we are a brilliant stock picker and that there is nothing wrong with our buy; it's the market that needs to wake up to our brilliance. Time will prove us right.

> Instead of correcting the error, we decide to double down.

And it is this commitment bias that ensures that once we've taken an action—once we've *committed* to our belief or our hypothesis—we naturally tend to become even more confident in this belief. We've done this; now we'll prove we were right.

Still, I firmly believe we are our own masters—each of us—and such biases can be overcome. Certainly, there are various non-stationary, truly stochastic situations where predicting future outcomes is fraught with error. The stock market, climate and weather, earthquakes/tsunamis—these are just a handful of such examples.

But in our financial lives, what we earn, save, spend—these are much more in our control. Those of us with greater resources can afford more hiccups in such areas—but the poor cannot. So, I believe an essential component in all of this is that we must do more, much more, to help those less fortunate among us to more clearly understand how their actions can do them so much harm; and what steps are available to them to gain better control.

Moreover, I believe it is incumbent on the rest of us—on business and society—to provide the poor with more tools and options.

The Poor Have Less Room to Err

Let's expand on this. Similar forms of errors harm different sectors of the population to very different degrees. The poor in particular have little leeway for errors that would have seemingly no effect on the well-to-do.

The poor live on the edge. They have much less margin for error. The sixteen-year-old son of a $250K per year business executive, just weeks after earning his driver's license, Snapchats while driving, which leads to a minor accident. A leased car, comprehensively insured, is towed to the shop by AAA with no added charge; a loaner car takes its place. The inconvenience to the family is minor, although to the minor in question, losing driving privileges for a month may seem the end of the world.

But consider the family from the south side of the tracks. A single mother needs her car to get to and from her two part-time jobs. Thankfully, the vehicle is paid off—as are most eleven-year-old cars—but this financially strained family can afford only basic liability coverage.

So, when struck by another motorist, her bare-bones insurance covers neither the cost of the tow nor a temporary loaner. The cost of the repair will eventually be covered, but in the meantime the cost of taking an Uber or a taxi each way represents a significant chunk of this woman's earnings for any shift. The family goes on alert: tight days ahead.

Then matters go still further South. As it turns out, the other motorist was uninsured. Certainly, they will be found liable for the damages in court, eventually. But good luck making a collection in this lifetime. And meanwhile, an already struggling small family comes face-to-face with an absolutely crippling repair bill. Decisions, decisions: pay the rent, eat, or fix the car?

> Decisions, decisions: pay the rent, eat, or fix the car?

A common, ordinary error, such as a minor car accident, will certainly be an inconvenience for anyone, but it can be a serious, even financially devastating problem for someone who is living paycheck to paycheck, with no margin for error. Imagine what it's like to need a title loan just to pay an auto repair bill—that is, if one can even find a loan company to lend against a vehicle already in the shop.

A fine balance exists in the world of spending. Error and inconsistency is everywhere in life. But the degree of suffering these errors produce is a function of our financial position—our margin for error. A 10 percent increase in cost to a well-to-do family can be easily cushioned with other savings or assets, or with a credit line or even a credit card. For the relatively well-off, error is not a catastrophe; it is simply a nuisance.

But, for the relatively poor, any surprising or unexpected cost—perhaps something so simple as a fall in the home and a trip to the emergency room—can precipitate enormous stress. How can a family with no savings—and a budget that features less than $200 or $300 in discretionary funds—sustain an unexpected expense of $500, $1,000, or more? Those living at the margin exist in a constant state of severe financial risk.

> For the relatively well-off, error is not a catastrophe; it is simply a nuisance.

Enter the Predator

The accidental consequences of accidental errors are significant enough. But the world is full of predators, seeking their own profit by capitalizing on our errors. These data miners and ad executives are very good at what they do. They know whom to target and how to appeal to their more impulsive desires. At its heart, of course, this is just good old caveat-emptor capitalism. It's free enterprise, writ large, and who could quarrel with that?

But does free enterprise really know no shame? So many business models today are built on the profits that can be gained by actively seeking out the slips and missteps of others, or even encouraging them. Certain landlords, for example, build in substantial fees for late rent payments. Certainly, these owners can claim that they are accepting a relatively high credit risk and thus should be entitled to high fees when they aren't paid on time. But a $50 or $75 penalty can equate to a full day or more of labor for the less well-off in our society.

And just stop to think about credit card lenders, cellular providers, cable companies, and electric utilities, and how many vehicles they deploy to tack on late fees, reconnection charges, and other penalties. Overdraft fees at a retail bank add still more insult to this already painful injury. At what point are these businesses actively *hoping* that their customers will foul up—that

For the poor, there are no minor financial binds.

they will err—so that profit margins can grow? Perhaps financial services companies should be required to post warnings and disclaimers such as those required for selling prescription drugs.

And what about "lifestyle" business models that convert the unaffordable $500 fifty-inch flat-screen television into an easy-to-budget $19.99 (plus tax) weekly payment, totaling $800 over the complete ten-month life of the contract? But don't be late with each weekly payment, or there'll be an additional usurious $15 late fee. Do the poor understand the deal they are striking, or are such bargains made in error?

Payday loans. Title loans. For the poor, there are no minor financial binds. So many are just one minor misstep from hunger or homelessness. And when those hunger pangs kick in, what are they willing to pay in terms of an interest rate to a predatory lender?

When you're crossing the desert, think what you'd pay for a glass of water. An arm and a leg for the first jug. But once you've been satiated, what would you pay for the next jug? Very little, if at all. You are no longer experiencing the extreme stress of thirst. The interest rate and other charges imposed on short-term loans (like payday loans) are scandalously high for the same reason: because those who must resort to this kind of product are stuck in a financial desert, and any thirst at all can be excruciating when the need is urgent.

Probably more often than we can appreciate, the poor person does recognize the harshness of this financial

Ignorance is not the issue; desperation is.

penalty. Ignorance is not the issue; desperation is. And when the rent is due, when the car breaks down, when the baby needs medicine—there are often no better, less costly options available, which is the only reason there is any kind of "demand" for these kinds of predatory products in the first place.

How Many Hours of My Life Will This Cost?

The well-to-do don't sweat the small stuff.

It's a typical day for our high-value freelance gig worker. This morning they see a $25 fee striking their bank account as their overseas client issues a wire transfer. Celebrating with a pair of $180 concert tickets, the $90 in tacked-on "convenience" fees may seem irritating, but it is, after all, Madonna touring with Lady Gaga (two of my favorite acts). So far, that's $115 in added fees, and we haven't even begun thinking about Starbucks, a sandwich for lunch, and dinner probably at that Greek place. A few hundred bucks barely dents this skilled professional's disposable income.

Turn to the lower-income hourly worker. Our bank account balance remains chronically well under the $1,500 average required for a free checking account, so there's $12 out the window every month (in 2018 over $6 billion was charged to consumers simply for the privilege of having a bank account). The subway fare is another $2.50 each way, so there's another $5 gone in an instant. There's free coffee at work if we're lucky; and lunch can be less than $5 if we pack our own or choose wisely in fast food. But what if we need a pain reliever, or cold medicine, or heel inserts for our aching feet? Before we know it, we've racked up fees and costs that easily consume a third or more of our take-home pay—and we've yet to think about how much of what we made today will need to go to pay our rent, smartphone, health insurance, and Netflix bills.

Yet again, it is the poorest among us who *must* be alert to all the risks and costs that could annihilate the household budget. Higher-wage earners have a vastly greater cushion—so they don't have to bother sweating the daily, dollars-and-cents details of their spending.

But the poor? They *must* know—and they do know—almost exactly how much they can spend on any given day. And on any days that those limits are breached, they also know they'll have to cut back on other days. Are their brains wired differently? Does this constant mental arithmetic change them?

And when limits are seriously breached, when errors are made, when accidents happen, the poor have precious few places to turn other than to usurious sources—i.e., the "usual suspects" in the crime of exploiting the desperate: predatory loans, late fees, overdraft charges.

Zero cash in checking? Time to comb through pockets, drawers, and seat cushions and head to the nearest Coinstar (where they incur another 9–10 percent or so in fees). Or . . . to the title loan center.

Society, it seems to me, should take more time to consider what can be done to provide the poorest among us with better options— options that cause less anguish and provide greater control. Options that do a better job of protecting them from the desperation that makes them such easy prey for the unscrupulous abusers of free-market capitalism.

Learn

The saying "consistency is the virtue of an ass" is commonly attributed to Ralph Waldo Emerson. Then in *Hillbilly Elegy*,[16] a book about growing up poor in rural Appalachia, J. D. Vance tells us that, while society may indeed bear a degree of responsibility to help the poor, the poor themselves cannot always blame their lot on mere circumstances.

Indeed, we may err consistently; the poor may be poor (or poorer) because they have a habit of making bad choices, such as renting chrome rims or contracting for the newest iPhone the moment it hits the market. But we also know that we can learn and improve. So, what can we do to help the poor? What can we do to educate the poor? We don't have to be horrible at golf forever; we don't have to repeat our mistakes in poverty.

As Lord John Maynard Keynes once remarked, "When my information changes, I alter my conclusions. What do you do, sir?"[17]

---

16 J. D. Vance, *Hillbilly Elegy: A Memoir of a Family and Culture in Crisis* (New York: HarperCollins, 2016).

17 Quoted in Paul Samuelson, "The Keynes Centenary," *The Economist* 287 (1983), 19.

■ IN PRACTICE

- In what areas might you—or your company's strategies—be subject to commitment bias?
- How many of your lower-wage employees are one paycheck away from financial duress?
- How many of your employees are already on the treadmill of short-term loans; title loans?
- Could any of this be having a negative impact on your business?

> In personal finances, too, having "guardrails" means errors aren't destructive but, instead, instructive.
>
> SAFWAN SHAH

Chapter Four

Revisiting the Laffer Curve

Can we better understand and optimize the time value of money as it relates to our lower-income workers?

- *Understanding optimization of taxation: the Laffer Curve*
- *Financial tolls and penalties: understanding the "Fin-Tax"*
- *Predatory Fin-Tax: striking hardest at the least resilient*
- *Even the IMF is a predatory lender*
- *Today's financial technology (fintech) exacerbates financial duress*
- *The role of time within the Fin-Tax*
- *Employers: understanding + inaction = complicity*

▦ ▦ ▦

You may or may not love his politics, but you should respect his wit and delivery. In "There They Go Again," a *New York Times* opinion piece penned in February 1993, former President Ronald Reagan took the opportunity to directly criticize the proposed tax policies of the newly inaugurated President Bill Clinton.

Reagan wrote:

> Just as positive signs of economic recovery are appearing,
> Mr. President, please don't blow it. Although it goes back
> well before the 1980s, may I offer you the advice of the 14th
> century Arab historian Ibn Khaldun, who said: "At the begin-
> ning of the empire, the tax rates were low and the revenues
> were high. At the end of the empire, the tax rates were high
> and the revenues were low." And, no, I did not personally
> know Ibn Khaldun, although we may have had some friends
> in common![18]

The Origins of the Laffer Curve

How is it that Reagan the author knew so much about Khaldun's
work? More than likely it was through Arthur Laffer, a key member
of Reagan's Economic Policy Board. Recall that, in a meeting with
President Reagan, Laffer famously scribbled his core idea on a
cocktail napkin—that there is a tax rate somewhere between 0 percent and 100 percent that delivers the optimal tax revenue. Known
today as the Laffer Curve, the economist was always transparent about the real inspiration for the
concept, a philosopher still guiding us
from medieval Tunisia.

Another way of describing the Laffer Curve or its effect is to say that the
more tax is incurred by any activity,
the less of that activity will likely take
place. Raise the tax by an increment,
and you will gain more revenue, but
the amount of taxable activity will also
decrease by an increment. Keep raising the rate, and activity will
eventually decline faster than revenue increases. So, if it can be

> Another way of
> describing the Laffer
> Curve or its effect is
> to say that the more
> tax is incurred by any
> activity, the less of
> that activity will likely
> take place.

---

18 Ronald Reagan, "There They Go Again," *New York Times*, February 18, 1993.

divined, there is also a theoretical rate of taxation that will optimize tax revenues. With respect to the personal income tax, would this rate be 28 percent? Or 70 percent? Or maybe 15 percent? And does the magnitude of this optimal rate remain somewhat constant, or will it tend to vary over time?

While we probably cannot universally agree on what this specific optimal rate is, we can't disagree that it must exist, somewhere between 0 percent and 100 percent.

But here's the question I really wish to pose: Can we draw an analogy between the optimization principal inherent in the Laffer Curve and the plight of the poorer segments of our own society, as they face the costs and difficulties of navigating their more precarious financial lives? Is there a "Laffer Curve" solution to the issue of abusive finance charges? Or if not a solution, is there at least a lesson to be learned?

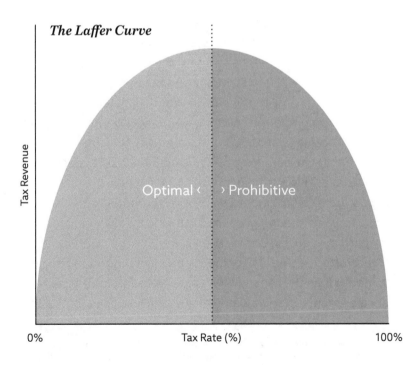

Understanding the Fin-Tax

Start first with all of the fees and penalties incurred by the working poor—let's call this a financial tax or "Fin-Tax." The Fin-Tax isn't something imposed by any government, but, rather, it's the collection of financial tolls and penalties that our lower-income workers experience on an almost daily basis, solely because they have little if any margin for error in their financial dealings. These are the kinds of fees and costs that the well-off almost never incur, because their own financial situation is not so vulnerable to the minor ups and downs of life.

For example? Consider the simplest and most basic financial service: a bank account. For most of us, this is one product that banks provide with no additional fees, recognizing they'll make their money on the deposit float and transaction fees that the account will produce, coupled with the other charges here and there, such as the fees they collect from merchants each time we swipe our plastic cards.

But for the poor? For starters, 57 percent of Americans have less than $1000 in their savings.[19] Individually, such meager deposits and transaction flows generate substantially less value from float or fees to the banks. Whether determined by science or simply competitive norm, banks typically require an average monthly balance of $1,500 or so to qualify for a free checking account. Others, the working poor, are debited $12–$15 per month in service fees. This is a financial tax.

> 57 percent of Americans have less than $1000 in their savings.

Recognize also that many cannot even organize their lives well enough to open a bank account at all—hence the prepaid card, check-cashing industry, and an even stiffer Fin-Tax.

Overdrafts? Better-off segments usually bring in more cash each month than they spend, or in many instances they have zero-balance accounts that draw down cash from savings, brokerage

---

19 Cameron Huddleston, "More Than Half of Americans Have Less Than $1,000 in Savings in 2017," GoBankingRates, September 12, 2017, https://www.gobanking rates.com/saving-money/half-americans-less-savings-2017/.

accounts, or other sources as needed. The poor? When they overdraw their checking account by a penny, even for a millisecond, they will be charged the infamous "NSF" (non-sufficient funds)

Overdrafts? Better-off segments usually bring in more cash than they spend.

fee—something generally running to about $35 per transaction. In fact, as of June 2017, the top ten retail banks in the US all charge NSF fees between $34 and $36 per transaction.[20] NSF fees represent a very costly Fin-Tax hitting those with the fewest financial resources the hardest.

Slow to pay the smartphone, heating, cable, or electric bill? Getting yourself current on an overdue bill will cost you a service fee, or a late charge, or perhaps a reconnection fee. Yet another Fin-Tax for the ones who can least afford it, as the rest of us, of course, are on autopay and rarely give such concerns a second thought.

From here, the rate of Fin-Tax only worsens. Often enticed by extremely attractive offers—including low introductory rates, or zero interest for balance transfers—the working poor can easily find themselves overwhelmed with credit card debt and interest. The wealthy among us? We may use credit cards, too, primarily to earn rewards points with our favorite airlines. Nonetheless, most of us still pay our balances in full each month, or nearly so.

All told, with respect to lower-income workers, our free-enterprise system has spawned entire industries that are organized almost exclusively for the purpose of levying and collecting the most Fin-Tax possible from those with the least ability to avoid it. For example, as reported by NerdWallet,[21] the Consumer Financial Protection Bureau (CFPB) "is investigating the $8 billion rent-to-own industry and related companies over questions about unfair, deceptive and abusive practices." NerdWallet research suspects

---

20 Spencer Tierney, "Overdraft Fees: Compare What Banks Charge," NerdWallet, August 10, 2018, https://www.nerdwallet.com/blog/banking/overdraft-fees-what-banks-charge/.

21 "Rent-A-Center Is Under Investigation for Credit Scam Allegations," NerdWallet, November 13, 2017, http://www.dontwasteyourmoney.com/rent-center-investigation-credit-scam-allegations/.

the industry is fraught with flaws ranging from POS systems that fail to accurately post transactions (plunging accounts into default unnecessarily) to workers "pocketing" cash payments along with aggressive collection policies.

Predatory Fin-Tax

So, in general, the Fin-Tax is what people are charged for the "privilege" of being financially desperate.

But are rent-to-own businesses or payday lenders providing a needed service? Do pawnbrokers and subprime credit cards offer anything of value at all for consumers? Demand proves that they are; they do. But the service fees and high rates of interest are tolls that are paid almost exclusively by the poorest in society, the ones whose desperation makes them the most vulnerable.

> Fin-Tax is what people are charged for the "privilege" of being financially desperate.

So, just how high is this Fin-Tax? First, look solely at bank overdraft fees—a fast-growing cottage industry within banks. According to Moebs Services, such fees reached $34.3 billion in 2017. The average fee of an overdraft has increased by 50 percent from $20 to $30. Recognize that overdraft programs require an opt-in from users; otherwise, their ATM debit cards would simply be declined. But serial "overdrafters" wind up spending $450 more on such fees, each year, relative to other customers, according to an agency press release.[22] In fact, a mere 9 percent of customers account for 79 percent of total overdraft fees.

So, who are these repeat offenders paying the vast majority of NSF penalties? Before going deeper into the report, we were already laying odds that the bulk would be lower-income workers, struggling to make ends meet. And we weren't disappointed, as the

---

22 Consumer Financial Protection Bureau, "CFPB Unveils Prototypes of 'Know Before You Owe' Overdraft Disclosure Designed to Make Costs and Risks Easier to Understand," August 4, 2017, https://www.consumerfinance.gov/about-us/newsroom/cfpb-unveils-prototypes-know-you-owe-overdraft-disclosure-designed-make-costs-and-risks-easier-understand/.

report goes on to say that frequent overdrafters tend to be "vulnerable, with lower daily balances and lower credit scores than people who do not overdraft as often."[23]

But now let's pull back and look at Fin-Tax of all categories across the full spectrum of society. A report from the Center for Financial Services Innovation (CFSI) estimates that the poor are paying approximately $170 billion per year in various fines, penalties, and interest charges that the rest of us rarely encounter.[24]

> A mere 9 percent of customers account for 79 percent of the overdraft fees.

Now, let's be conservative in our estimate, making sure to capture all of those who might be contributing to this Fin-Tax pool, and say that, of the approximately 140 million currently in the workforce, two-thirds or 80 million encounter such fees.

Evenly distributing this burden across this broad segment totals $2,000 plus per worker, not an insignificant amount by any means. But then recognize that this is a burden being borne by the poorest among us. The realization is that societal Fin-Tax, disproportionately levied on the poor, is an enormous source of financial duress/stress levied upon those least equipped to afford it.

Before we move on, let me just be sure you understand my position when it comes to the Fin-Tax. In case you haven't guessed, I'm opposed to it. And I'm also opposed to all the societal, governmental, and business practices that have led a great free-market democracy such as ours to impose this terrible, unjust burden on its lower-income citizens. A big part of my life's work has been oriented around helping to reduce or eliminate financial suffering wherever feasible. And the Fin-Tax accounts for a big part of this suffering.

---

23 Ibid.

24 Thereas Schmall and Eva Wolkowitz, *2016 Financially Underserved Market Size Study* (Center for Financial Services Innovation, November 2016), https://cfsinnovation.org/wp-content/uploads/2016/11/2016-Financially-Underserved-Market-Size-Study_Center-for-Financial-Services-Innovation.pdf.

Why Inflict Desperation?

The market for financial products and services that impose a Fin-Tax is borne out of desperation—desperation on the part of the consumers of these products.

And why call it Fin-Tax? To my thinking, as Americans, we love to reduce taxes. There is joy to be derived from tax reduction; taxation is the enemy, hampering innovation and economic activity. So, by referring to these tolls and penalties endured primarily by the poor as a form of tax, I am hoping we can win more people to our cause. And, as much data as has already been mentioned, we actually could spend the rest of this book presenting additional evidence. For now, let me say simply: I hope the term Fin-Tax helps build support for us all to work together finding a cure.

Now, let's relate the desperation caused by Fin-Tax to the Laffer Curve. Laffer presents a model that can help society and government optimize tax rates and government revenues. But what about Fin-Tax? Is there an optimal amount of Fin-Tax that society can and should bear?

And, as we wrestle with the question, the realization takes hold that traditional taxes and Fin-Tax are not directly analogous. Fin-Tax is a transfer of value from private citizens to businesses. It is not collected for the greater good, but rather for the good of corporations or in many cases the good of mom-and-pop title loan stores or pawnshops—Fin-Tax entrepreneurs—at the expense of those working from paycheck to paycheck.

> Fin-Tax is a transfer of value from private citizens to businesses.

The questions become: What is the optimal amount of Fin-Tax that society and industry should inflict upon—collect from—the poor? If we allow our free-enterprise economy to squeeze more and more from this already poverty-stricken segment, at what point does the desperation rise *too* high? Is there a point at which the misery index will spike and the social fabric fail?

The question isn't why would we ever want to test the societal limits of tolerance for the Fin-Tax, a plainly inequitable and despicable additional penalty for being poor. Rather, the question is: Why would we intentionally want to inflict any Fin-Tax at all?

The IMF as a Payday Lender

There is no question that payday lenders, rent-to-own providers, title loan companies, pawnbrokers, and similar predatory operators are in fact providing a service that can be a true life-saver for those in need. And no doubt the proprietors of such businesses believe in their hearts that they are helping their customers.

Similarly, when a credit card or utility company charges a late fee, or when a bank charges an NSF fee, these entities likely feel they have every right to charge what rents they can in order to maximize their own value and protect their own interests. They are every bit as much a part of Adam Smith's invisible hand as are the auto companies assembling cars in Georgia or the AI-focused businesses remapping Silicon Valley.

> But there comes a point when natural, economic self-interest becomes entirely too selfish.

But there comes a point when natural, economic self-interest becomes entirely too selfish. Take a look at the International Monetary Fund (IMF), a well-intentioned quasi-governmental entity whose mission, according to the website, is "working to foster global monetary cooperation, secure financial stability, facilitate international trade, promote high employment and sustainable economic growth, and reduce poverty around the world."[25]

Noble indeed. So why then did historian/anthropologist David Graeber go so far as to describe the IMF as the world's "debt enforcers—the high finance equivalent of the guys who come to break your legs"?[26]

---

25 "About the IMF," International Monetary Fund, https://www.imf.org/en/About.

26 David Graeber, *Debt: The First 5000 Years* (Brooklyn: Melville House Publishing, 2011), 2.

As Graeber tells the story, OPEC nations in the 1970s were flooded with newfound cash—as were their banking counterparts. So, the banks set about looking for new ways to invest all this cash, and one of the most common answers became: lend to Third World countries. Of course, evil dictators running corrupt societies meant that all such sovereign borrowing was quickly funneled into private accounts, leaving the host nations destitute.

Forget about the question of whether or not the peoples of such nations should be held accountable for the actions of their criminal leadership, or whether banks should be repaid regardless of where the original monies disappeared to. Where it all led was to the Third World debt crisis of the '80s and '90s.

But not to worry: to the rescue came the IMF. Yes, these nations needed help: hospitals, schools, roads, water systems, wastewater treatment, electrical grids. And certainly, the IMF was prepared to lend a hand, pushing as much cash as it could muster into these needy nations in the form of new loans.

> Essentially, the IMF became the payday lender of last resort to the Third World and, in the process, levied a new Fin-Tax on the world's poorest people.

But in return? Two words: structural reform. This is what the IMF required. Tax your people just a bit more. Raise those municipal electricity rates just a few cruzeiros/rupees/pesos/local dollars more. In return for new money, the IMF converted a number of these developing economies into its own ongoing revenue stream.

And who pays? Again, the poorest, most vulnerable sectors of society are the ones feeling the most pain. It is an international Fin-Tax. Essentially, the IMF became the payday lender of last resort to the Third World and, in the process, levied a new Fin-Tax on the world's poorest people.

Did the IMF recognize how it was hamstringing so many economies? Did it see what it was doing to the poorest citizens of these corrupt but destitute nations? Most likely not. The corrupt got the money, and the poor got the Fin-Tax.

If you think this story of international politics is too far afield from the topic at hand, let me call your attention to the otherwise harmless, well-intended payroll practices of today's employers. The batch process may be dead in nearly every other human endeavor, but modern employers cling to the batch process with respect to their payroll practices with the fervor that a fifteenth-century scribe might cling to his quill pen when offered a computer and keyboard.

And, in the process, employers are unintentionally—but no less viciously—constricting the just and right flow of value to their lowest-paid workers. It may simply be that business owners don't recognize the harm they are inflicting. I like to believe that anyway. How could it be otherwise?

Unintentional Predators?

For these and related reasons, I strongly believe that the business community at large, and employers in particular, need to reassess their payroll practices in light of their unintended consequences. *Not* using already widely available technologies for the purpose of easing the burdens on lower- and middle-income workers shows a lack of care, unintentional or not.

To illustrate, let's next talk about some of today's already advanced but still fast-evolving financial technologies, or fintech. Fintech might be described as the entire collection of point of sale, mobile, and other payment platforms as well as credit facilities, online purchase tracking, loyalty programs—every byte-enabled, real-time, cloud-powered, AI-guided financial tool at the daily disposal of today's more innovative businesses.

At fintech's heart: data, and I do mean vast caches of data. These firms collect, inspect, categorize, analyze, and act upon every precious morsel of data they can find. And to what end? The truth is, every algorithm, every sensor, every trigger in the fintech world is designed wholly and solely to maximize

Every trigger in the fintech world is designed wholly and solely to maximize sales.

sales and profits for the owners of said processes and technologies. Phrased another way: Everyone is using fintech to build a Laffer-like optimization of the value of people. Technology is being used to monetize individuals for the optimal benefit of the owners of fintech.

Of course this is so. Maximization of profit was as much a goal of the local shop or saloon keeper of the early 1900s as it is today for all businesses, large and small. Both fintech and the Fin-Tax arise from a highly technological and networked economy in which each participant plays as many cards as they can to further their own economic self-interest.

If you're a credit card provider, your offer is designed with features that incentivize spending. Your systems tell you when to text or email a special offer—and to which customers—to drive the most possible purchases. Your data-driven insights, enhanced by sophisticated algorithms and machine learning, are uncannily successful in shaping commercial behaviors.

At the same time, these processes and algorithms are incredibly effective at detecting patterns to exploit. How, for example, can we maximize revenue? One way is to make certain the software is clever enough to derive benefit from a customer's potentially smallest failures. Late payment fees, the machines notice, can be a remarkably profitable business line. But be careful in setting the amount of the fee. Too little, and the company loses out on revenue; too much, and the customers begin taking greater care to avoid such surcharges. Profiting from error is a delicate business and needs to be cautiously optimized.

> Profiting from error is a delicate business and needs to be cautiously optimized.

Fintech in and of itself is not evil—fintech just does its job. Certainly, businesses want to provide value to their customers. And customers have the choice to transact with a business or not—isn't that correct? Actually, when it comes to financial services, maybe not. Today, you pretty much *have* to have a banking account and be able to use a debit card or write a check. Some may still live in the cash economy, but the vast majority of us are using today's tools. The irony is, however, that those with the least ability to pay for such tools are the ones that pay the most for them.

Moreover, business and society seem not to notice the incredibly damaging, unintended consequences of fintech unfettered. Too much of anything can be a bad thing. A scalpel in the hands of a skilled surgeon can be life-saving. But if the surgery never ends, it becomes death by a thousand cuts.

When so much Fin-Tax is collected from segments so ill-equipped to cope with the burden, the level of desperation skyrockets. Whole tiers of workers barely making ends meet, paycheck to paycheck, cannot concentrate on their work. They don't sleep well; they consume greater quantities of alcohol or drugs to cope; they arrive late to work or not at all. They make mistakes while working. And, like Great Britain's "Brexit," they vote for change.

Stress multiplies, and desperation builds: Fin-Tax-exacerbated poverty begets still greater desperation. So, a massive segment of society that with just a modicum of relief could become significantly more productive instead becomes trapped in a seemingly endless cycle—resentful and resistant, but still powerless. Perhaps without even realizing, many employers are squeezing the humanity out of their workers.

> Perhaps without even realizing, many employers are squeezing the humanity out of their workers.

Time

Time, of course—a recurring theme throughout this book—plays a critical role in the oppression of the desperate.

As the founder and CEO of PayActiv, I can attest that time may be the single most important part of our own journey. Paying people more? That's a very different discussion. Tax people less? That's also not my ask. My ask is simple and very much in control of the employers: pay people on a timelier basis—the kind of timely basis on which almost all other business processes already operate, given today's technologies. Give your workers convenient access to what they've already earned. Time matters. Maybe not to folks making six figures, but it matters to the 75 million hourly workers.

So much of the pain of Fin-Tax is driven by time. For those who live paycheck to paycheck, life and work is an endless cycle of binging and fasting. Imagine, a week from the next pay day: funds are low and yet the rent is due, there's no gas in the tank, and there's very little food in the freezer. Anxiety and stress are high; few if any of life's pleasures can be purchased to help alleviate the anguish.

Finally, payday arrives. And what is the natural response following a prolonged period of enforced deprivation? Celebration! Binging on the consumption of unnecessary luxuries, as well as restoring safety stocks, like gas and food, which had fallen to negative levels. Within days, the worker living paycheck to paycheck will often have gorged on consumption and ended up right back where they were prior to having been paid, in the same way that a calorie-counting dieter might ruin two weeks' worth of weight loss with a single evening's ill-considered feasting on chips and chocolates.

> Time is not the friend of someone who has no margin for error.

Time is not the friend of someone who has no margin for error.

The story for business itself, however, is almost the mirror opposite. Businesses are economically clever, and demonstrate a keen awareness of the financial value of time at nearly every turn. Companies run sophisticated treasury functions whose cash management processes maximize the present value of their assets. Sales terms are written in such a way as to accelerate the rate at which cash is received by the business, while purchase agreements slow the business's payments to vendors. Discount rates, netting, pooling, zero-balance "sweep" accounts, and myriad other tools and techniques ensure that a business perfectly optimizes the timing of its cash flows to yield the maximum value.

Businesses know that, when it comes to cash flow, time matters. But, when it comes to their employees' daily lives, apparently it doesn't.

Businesses have also put a great deal of thought into how they compensate their highest earning executives. Such employees are well aware of key issues such as the time value of money and the tax consequences, and the timing of executive compensation is often carefully engineered, with an eye on the calendar.

Lower-wage workers, however, are always paid "in arrears." The rationale offered most often by HR professionals is that it takes time to onboard a worker and get them into the payroll system. But once the system is up and running, why not pay the worker in full, up through the actual "as of" pay date? Well, here things get a bit murky. For some businesses, the reason seems to be that this is just the way it's always been done, and we see no reason to change (after all, it's not the managers in charge of the payroll process who are desperate for their pay).

Other companies have told me that, if they were to pay out in full, they would worry that some of their lower-wage workers might not show up for work again; so, paying in arrears is one tactic they can use to keep their workers tied to them, rather like a modern version of the company store.

Getting to Know You

It isn't clear today whether the notorious eighteenth-century tweet often misattributed to Marie Antoinette, *"Qu'ils mangent de la brioche"* (Let them eat cake!), and US Commerce Secretary Wilbur Ross's comment that furloughed workers in the longest government shutdown should take out loans indicated a lack of understanding of the plight of the poor or simply a disdain for the starving masses. Nor is it clear whether employers' current, antiquated payroll methods are the result of inattention and neglect or disdain for their lowest-paid workers.

One can only hope that the haves will develop greater understanding of (and empathy for) the have-nots.

But increasing levels of social connectedness and the availability of vast amounts of data seem to be creating a clearer two-way window between the haves and the have-nots. Certainly, the latter are able to see the remarkable luxuries enjoyed by the former: travel, lavish homes, remarkable toys, exorbitant salaries. One can only hope that the haves will develop greater understanding of (and empathy for) the have-nots.

The damage being inflicted on society's most vulnerable should be understood to be quite intentional.

Marie Antoinette may simply have been unaware. Wilbur Ross may just be ignorant. But today we are all more connected, and we know much more about the circumstances of others. We know the Uber driver is renting his time and vehicle to us out of need—and that this is very likely a secondary source of income (and, in comparison to what we as passengers likely earn, a relatively meager one). We also know that our waiter or waitress could be supporting a little boy or girl at home.

The question becomes: Knowing what we know today, do we tip a bit more? Do we pay a bit more? Do we share a bit more? Is social connectedness increasing our empathy? Or, as activist/author Eli Pariser puts things, are we prisoners of our own "filter bubbles,"[27] seeing only the facts we already know, and reading only the opinions we already agree with?

Isn't it time we do more for our workforce? It would cost employers very little to simply give workers easier and timely access to the fruits of their labors.

By continuing to withhold the earnings of lower-wage workers, skewing the timing of their payment to our own benefit, we increase the level of stress among the most vulnerable members of our society. Moreover, we cast these paycheck-to-paycheck workers into a financial purgatory, where they become easy prey for payday lenders and other rapacious financial actors.

As for the abused themselves, the low-income workers, I often wonder if matters haven't evolved into some sort of codependent relationship. The abused begins believing that they deserve the abuse: it is their fate and, being abused, this becomes a new normal.

---

27 Eli Pariser, *The Filter Bubble: How the New Personalized Web Is Changing What We Read and How We Think* (London: The Penguin Press, 2012).

Hence, overdrafts, late fees, rental flat screens, title loans, and other subprime credit transactions continue to flourish.

Employers, Where Is Your Outrage?

No one should be allowed to continue claiming ignorance of these facts. No one should sleep well at night, knowing that their own carefully crafted financial systems continue to subject their lowest-income, most vulnerable workers to a life of unnecessary financial stress.

No, the harm being caused should no longer be considered simply collateral damage from "business as usual." The damage being inflicted on society's most vulnerable should be understood to be quite intentional.

By their inaction, employers are saying that they *intentionally* withhold their workers' earnings, either as a means of retention or to avoid having to go to the trouble of changing their processes and adopting new, readily available (and dirt cheap) technologies. Or could it be that employers are seeking to act as a bank and earn a profit on the float, a profit that (to them) outweighs the costs in terms of employee anguish and emotional suffering? Or perhaps, withholding payment is simply a crude means of reducing absenteeism.

> When you, the business owner or manager, refuse employees timely access to their own compensation, given the technologies available today, you are inflicting harm with conscious intent.

Whatever the case, businesses may feel they're doing something wise, when in fact they're actually inflicting tremendous harm. This should no longer be considered some sort of accidental consequence. When you, the business owner or manager, refuse employees timely access to their own compensation, given the technologies available today, you are inflicting harm with conscious intent.

You *know* they have no cake and they can't qualify for a loan. You know the batch is dead. **Why are you still inflicting such harm?**

■ IN PRACTICE

- What steps, if any, are you taking to evaluate your employees' financial well-being?
- Are you aware of the numbers of your employees using payday or title loans, renting their home furnishings, or making use of predatory financial services?
- To what degree might financial duress impact employee performance or your business's performance?
- How long do your employees have to wait before being paid?

*Relieved of Fin-Tax burdens, and with a system
to manage vital air supply, employees have the freedom
to explore opportunities.*

SAFWAN SHAH

> When humans feel undue stress, their faculties are diminished, and their focus and productivity suffer.

SAFWAN SHAH

Chapter Five

Sensitive Dependence on Initial Conditions

Where we are today doesn't always take into account how we got here: so, doesn't it make sense to pay closer attention to initial conditions?

- *Initial conditions: what they are and why it matters*
- *Poverty is relative*
- *Studies show that scarcity creates stressors that reduce IQ*
- *Practically speaking: let's level the playing field*
- *Are we "institutionalizing" workers?*
- *Let's remake education*

■ ■ ■

If you've been successful, you didn't get there on your own. I'm always struck by people who think, well, it must be because I was just so smart. There are a lot of smart people out there. It must be because I worked harder than everybody else. Let me tell you something—there are a whole bunch of hardworking people out there.

If you were successful, somebody along the line gave you some help. There was a great teacher somewhere in your life. Somebody helped to create this unbelievable American system that we have that allowed you to thrive. Somebody invested in roads and bridges.

If you've got a business—you didn't build that. Somebody else made that happen. The Internet didn't get invented on its own. Government research created the Internet so that all the companies could make money off the Internet.

The point is [. . .] that when we succeed, we succeed because of our individual initiative, but also because we do things together.

PRESIDENT BARACK OBAMA, July 13, 2012

⬛ ⬛ ⬛

I know the above statements arrived with great controversy. **So, let's agree immediately that, if you are a successful person today, no doubt you yourself are the key driving force behind that success**. Others, like your parents, teachers, or maybe a mentor or two along the way may have helped shape you. I know they did shape me. But ultimately, it is *you* with the drive to succeed.

As an entrepreneur myself, I believe that, yes, without an entrepreneur's own vision and drive, it is very likely their business would never exist, and if you work for others, your career might not exist without your own effort. No one is handing you your success. So, if nothing else, understand that I am a firm believer in the power of the individual to drive, influence, and deliver the results they desire. *Personal* accountability matters.

But the question I want to pose is this: Does *societal* accountability matter? How about businesses: are they accountable, beyond their owners or shareholders? To what degree do we as a society need to begin thinking more about our collective well-being?

Initial Conditions

Chaos theory talks of the vital or "sensitive" importance of initial conditions in understanding dynamic systems. Drop a sphere—a ball—onto a razor blade, and it may fall to the left or to the right. Unless the precise center of the ball's mass landed precisely on the blade's edge, there will be a bias to one side or the other. And, in real life, precision is a myth. It's an artificial construct. Was the ball spinning, which would introduce angular momentum? Was there a slight wind, or a tiny magnetic force involved? To reliably predict the path of the sphere, or to determine the cause for the sphere's movement after the fact, these along with so many other factors need to be taken into account.

Consider the degree to which who you are today is driven by where and to whom you happened to be born.

Initial conditions matter. And this is also true for how we develop as individuals. We don't always like to admit the full extent to which they matter. We like to believe the lion's share of who we are today is the result of our own hard work. And, indeed, it is true. I've said it: we all have a tremendous amount of influence and control over what we do with our own lives.

But at least consider the degree to which who you are today is driven by where and to whom you happened to be born. Let's start with your genetics. Someone could practice basketball, golf, or cricket as much as they like. However, without the same caliber of physical gifts as Michael Jordan, Tiger Woods, or Imran Khan (the great cricketer who is now the prime minister of Pakistan), they will never dunk like Jordan, putt like Woods, or bowl like Khan.

To some degree, the same goes for how handsome society

holds a man to be or how beautiful a woman is. Diet and work-outs may matter; so do skin and hair treatments and clothing and lighting. But, overall, if we exude those characteristics that society deems to be the most attractive, it is primarily a function due more to our genetics than to most other factors.

What about IQ—the nature-versus-nurture debate? Is a person's intellectual zenith/nadir established at birth, or is their environment the true empowering or limiting factor? To what degree can our natural talents be developed or debased, contingent on the circumstances of our upbringing?

IQ, attractiveness, athleticism—these and other personal variables can be improved upon through effort just as they can decay from neglect. But, absolutely, there are upper limits imposed by genetics. We are all dealt a hand by genetics, which we are left to play according to our own individual willingness and ability.

> A certain degree of randomness governs all of us.

A certain degree of randomness governs all of us. As it turns out, for instance, one of the key drivers in economic success is the zip code in which we are born. Without pointing to any specific research on the matter, common sense tells us that a child born and raised on the "wrong side of the tracks" faces challenges beyond those of the relatively more "well-to-do." Or take this basic test: which child faces more of an uphill battle, the one born to a refugee family in the midst of the Syrian civil war, or the one born to a hotelier in Nice?

Many took great offense to the words of President Obama I quoted at the beginning of this chapter. Entrepreneurs in particular zeroed in on the statement, "If you've got a business—you didn't build that." And, truth be told, though I appreciate the overall point, that particular statement in my own estimation rings a partial truth.

Entrepreneurs—owners—rise up every morning to build their businesses, knowing that they are taking the bulk of the risk. Therefore, there's a vast gulf between the mindset of a hired employee and that of an owner. Ultimately, any crisis is the owner's responsibility.

While hired employees, particularly great ones, might tackle crises that arise, the success of the business still ultimately resides with the owner. Countless hours invested by entrepreneurs or similarly entrepreneurial and advancement-minded workers mean that, indeed, the bulk of any success is the product of dogged hard work and the ability to take calculated risks.

But think for a moment. What if you—your body and its consciousness—had been delivered to war-torn Beirut, with infrastructure, healthcare, and schools crumbling around you, producing chronic insecurity in terms of basic food and shelter. Or maybe it's just the impoverished South side of Chicago, or Glasgow Shettleston, or the slums of Mumbai. If you're reading this book, you are likely a dogged hard worker, a survivor, a risk-taker, by nature. But the question is, how high would you have been able to climb in this life had your initial starting point been one of considerably greater poverty or much lesser opportunity?

> If you are reading this book you are likely a hard worker—a survivor—by nature.

Perceptions of Poverty

Having grown up in one of the world's most dangerous and poverty-stricken regions—more on that later—I have personally seen more than my share of unsettling situations. One story I could share to illustrate the vast gulf in initial conditions has to do with a person who worked for my family.

My family wasn't ultrarich. Maybe *well-off* is the right term. But we did have house help. Among them, Juma Khan, was someone who I was very fond off in my early teens while living in Quetta. Many years later he contacted my mother with a request. If it wasn't too much trouble, the next time I came home to visit, he would like to be informed so he could make a two-day train trip from Quetta to Karachi to see me.

As it turns out, a few months later I did visit Karachi, and Juma, now an old man, made the trek. Nearly blind, he wanted some help to get his eyesight restored, so I took him to the best eye doctor in the area. Once there, the doctor told me the condition was significantly more complicated than mere cataracts and that no matter what we did the odds were likely that Juma would be only slightly better off than he was already.

The doctor strongly suggested that, rather than pay his relatively high fee, we would be better off going to a subsidized clinic. Why? Paraphrasing, the doctor told me, "Because I don't believe he will see all that well, and since you will have paid so much for this, he will have higher expectations, and will likely only complain when these expectations aren't met."

I couldn't bear to tell this to Juma and instead gave him some money to go to a different doctor, which he did and his eyesight greatly improved. Now I share this story not to imply in any way that the prior doctor was a cruel person. Rather, what this example illustrates is how our perceptions of quality of life are affected by differences in wealth and standing. The same initial conditions.

> In the West, we are happy to spend significant sums on health care, even if the resulting improvement in quality of lifespan is only marginal.

In the West, we are happy to spend significant sums on health care, even if the resulting improvement in quality of life or lifespan is only marginal. In a poorer nation, to waste such precious resources for so little expected gain is strongly discouraged. For me, this experience sheds more light on the vast global variances in quality of life, based on initial conditions, and the bias that tends to accompany those conditions.

Scarcity Reduces IQ

Something else we've learned: financial duress consumes IQ. In *Scarcity: The New Science of Having Less and How It Defines Our Lives,* authors Sendhil Mullainathan and Eldar Shafir provide an array of illustrations of, well, just as the title explains. In one of the most intriguing examples, the two researchers headed out to a mall in New Jersey with one of their graduate students to examine the degree to which scarcity might impact decision-making.

Random subjects were given a battery of tests to measure cognitive control and fluid intelligence. But, in the midst of this IQ testing, participants were also asked to imagine that they had just been given a bill for car repair expenses totaling either a relatively minor $150 or a more substantial $1500.

To analyze the results, the researchers broke down the subjects based on their self-reported income levels. With respect to the $150 loss scenario, test performance remained consistent, whether rich or poor. But, when it came to the $1,500 loss scenario, something changed. Here, relatively well-to-do test takers saw little to no decay in the scores they achieved on the intelligence test, while, for participants living their lives with less income, scores fell significantly.

The conclusion: for the wealthy, whether the cost is $150 or $1,500, the issue is just another bump in the road. For the relatively poor? They, too, can manage a $150 loss, but a $1,500 "surprise" creates significant financial stress, interfering with their ability to focus, and resulting in a loss of, yes, IQ points.

Similar studies reached similar conclusions, when examining the mental faculties of farmers, pre- and post-harvest. Prior to harvest time, with seeds still in the ground and the perils of drought, insects, and general uncertainty still before them, cognitive tests revealed stress and inhibited performance. Post-harvest? Poise and sound decision-making returned, generating an additional thirteen IQ points.

These illustrations support what should be evident even without such studies. It is a readily accepted theory by psychologists that, no matter how smart any of us may be, there are still limits to how much we can process at one time. Just like your laptop is limited by its DRAM (dynamic random access memory)—which refers to how much memory is available to run active programs—our brains can only deal with so much at once.

For those of us who are wealthier? Bumps in the road like that

$1,500 car repair consume comparatively little DRAM. We don't sweat the small stuff and can thus focus on our work and lives. But, for those in or near poverty, something like that unexpected major car repair can easily lead to cognitive overload. Something that means little or nothing to a wealthier person can be cognitively crippling to a poor person.

Importantly, what this means is that the poor are much less likely to perform up to their full potential in life, simply because DRAM-draining financial duress is nearly omnipresent.

Why should we care? Today, nearly two-thirds of the global population is living in this bandwidth-impaired state. But just imagine if we could reduce even a fraction of this toxic stress. How much more productive could our workers become? How much more would they be able to produce and earn over their lives and careers? That's more than just a better workforce; it's a healthier consumer market. Bottom line, we need to do more to understand and help to improve their condition. It's in our own interest—*society*'s interest—to do so.

> More than a just better workforce, it's a healthier consumer market.

Practically Speaking: Let's Level the Playing Field

What if business and society were to begin taking a person's initial conditions as a variable to be included in an assessment of their skills, potential, and abilities? As it turns out, this is something that my uncle, professor Haroon Ahmed, a retired master of Corpus Christi College in Cambridge University, has been considering at length of late.

Not long ago I had the opportunity to join him for golf. We were at the Gog Magog golf course in Cambridge, and at one point as we were walking, he started to tell me his latest responsibility. As a professor, his life had, up until recently, focused primarily on research and teaching. But increasingly his role had become consultative, steering committees, board memberships, advisory roles, and so forth. Quite often, his role required him to help in talent recruitment and hiring decisions, selecting the best possible candidate for various senior positions at the organizations he helped. And this meant choosing from the crème de la crème in today's talent pools. In fact, at that moment he was engaged in interviewing a wide range of prominent, highly-experienced candidates for a senior position.

I thought for a few moments before congratulating my uncle. I told him, "Wow, this is a tremendous responsibility. The people that you choose, for whom you cast your vote, are going to have an impact on the organizations for decades to come. Because of your illustrious career, your experience and accomplishments, you are in the position that truly drives the future."

He smiled, thought it over, and then acknowledged by nodding. But then he added, "This is really hard."

"How so?" I asked.

Well, as it turned out, one of the key challenges was having so many remarkably qualified candidates and applicants. Because they all are so good, determining who really stands out—who will perform best in the role—is extremely difficult. Being inquisitive, I asked, "So what is your process?"

To my surprise, it was at this point that my uncle laid out an approach, taking initial conditions into full account. He said, if memory serves, "I use math. I take a time series approach. I don't look solely at where the candidates are today. Instead, I go back over their lives and resumes to see where they started. And then I create a journey, seeing what it took from where they started to where they are today."

We can all quibble on the precise parameters to enter into our grids. But let's say that today you are at level 8 in your life and career. Where did you start? Were you born into a level 5 household or a level 2? Without going into the detail of the calculus he applies, my uncle described two hypothetical candidates. One could be the son or daughter of a pair of well-heeled professionals. The other began life in a village outside of Shanghai. Both are now at comparable levels of achievement. But the question becomes: Should we presume the latter had far further to climb, led a more interesting life, navigated and overcame greater challenges? If x = one unit of accomplishment, the former rose $3x$ whereas the latter rose $6x$?

Such an approach turns a difficult human resources question into an engineering problem. Certainly, it creates a framework for comparing various people in the context of their initial conditions. But is it really fair? Well, who said the world was fair to begin with—IQs, looks, athleticism? But is this a sort of adjustment, a leveling mechanism, that society should routinely consider?

Institutionalizing a Workforce

Let me begin by saying, I love Walmart, Costco, Best Buy, Office Max, PetCo—you name any big-box retailer, and I have a great appreciation for what they've done for the consumer. The same applies to large grocery chains, fast-food purveyors, and even mass market regional, national, or global restaurant franchises. And I have no wish to single out any company or industry for misdeeds or lack of social consciousness. But it just so happens that these and other retailers and restauranteurs reside squarely in the path of a technology-caused megatrend that is only now coming into clearer focus: the ever-worsening prospects for low-skilled workers.

Industries that traditionally hire loads of relatively unskilled labor are being transformed. Take retail: digital commerce has already turned many once lucrative malls into comparative ghost towns. And having achieved so much success selling electronics, clothing, and similar wares, the action is now moving into groceries, with digital leviathan Amazon acquiring Whole Foods for over $13.7 billion in cash—and already slashing the prices of its offerings (significantly reducing the market capitalization of its competitors in the process).

Now add robots and automation to the list. Go to any major airport today and notice fewer behind-the-counter people, as everyone is asked to check in via the self-service kiosks. There are fewer wait staff at restaurants, fewer retail clerks in department stores, and fewer attendants at newsstands. And what is to become of the nearly 11 million US workers who operate vehicles for a living, once the promise of self-driving cars and trucks is fully-realized?

Disruption has been around for centuries—ask any former buggy whip maker or video store owner. But the pace and scale of disruption today is beyond remarkable. Moreover—it is poised to break like a tsunami across the whole of the low-skilled workforce.

So how does this relate to a sensitive dependence on initial conditions? To my mind, it is time that society— and this includes business and industry—begins focusing more attention and resources on preparing its workforce for a future of continuous change. For whatever combination of reasons—be it their zip code, their relative IQ, an abusive parent, drugs or alcohol—society includes a substantial portion of low-skilled workers.

> Disruption has been around for centuries.

And what has happened, traditionally, is that such workers have been trained only to do particular jobs. That is, a big-box retailer trains its workers to do *this* job and little else. The same is true of the fast-food and fast casual restaurant chains. Certainly, there will be workers who stand out and are thus put on some sort of fast track, learning a wider range of tasks and skills—culled from the herd to become future managers. But, for the most part, workers have always learned just enough to keep doing their jobs.

So, what happens when the Amazons of this world succeed with their efficiency-focused business models? Already, prices are down at Whole Foods, but the group is also expected to use technology and other process improvements to slash staffing levels.

What happens when the big-box stores leave town, the cashiers and wait staff are supplanted by terminals, and the forklift operators and taxi or Uber/Lyft drivers are replaced by robots? So many institutionalized workers will become relatively helpless, unable to shift to new industries or endeavors because of the narrow focus of their training.

An era of disruption requires that we begin training our workforce to be more flexible.

An era of disruption requires that we begin training our workforce to be more flexible. Certainly, we must provide training needed for the role at hand. But businesses and society need to do more to broaden such training.

As for business executives, I submit there is much that can be done not only to instill greater flexibility in workers but also to generate greater productivity, loyalty, and value. Businesses that broaden the training available—perhaps teaching workers about personal financial management or technology—will find they have a significantly happier, more committed and capable workforce.

Let's Remake Education

While businesses themselves would likely benefit greatly from providing workers with such training, this is also something that should be taken up by local government. In fact, while we're at it, let's think about what could be done to improve the quality of education in general.

Rethinking Higher Education

In his June 12, 2005 commencement speech at Stanford, Steve Jobs talked about his experience at Reed College and how colleges today are in many ways too rigid. Too many of the required classes, he explained, seemed pointless and were of no interest to Jobs. Recognizing that his attendance was meanwhile draining his parents' savings, six months into his college experience, he dropped out.

Though no longer on the official rolls, Jobs stayed on at the school as a vagrant. He soon took to sleeping in friends' dorm rooms, collecting soda cans and bottles for their nickel deposit value, and hiking seven miles on Sundays for one good free meal a week at a Buddhist monastery. Though it was "pretty scary at the time," Jobs says that "looking back, it was one of the best decisions

I ever made. The minute I dropped out I could stop taking the required classes that didn't interest me, and begin dropping in on the ones that looked interesting."[28]

As it turns out, a calligraphy class unofficially "audited" by Jobs delved into the subtleties and intricacies of lettering and font design. Jobs noted that at the time "none of this had even a hope of any practical application in my life."[29] Nonetheless, the payoff came ten years later during the design of one of Apple's most revolutionary products. As Jobs explains, "If I had never dropped in on that single course in college, the Mac would have never had multiple typefaces or proportionally spaced fonts."[30]

Revisiting Public Education

Where do our leaders come from? Which schools are the best at preparing our best and brightest for going out into the world, driving innovation and advancement among our most vital institutions? Okay, so we'll throw out a few discussion starters. Is it Carnegie Mellon? MIT? Oxford? HEC Paris? Cambridge? Stanford? How about Harvard or Yale?

No doubt, we could write a series of books on what should be done to renovate university educations. This is to say nothing of the various corporate innovations, like GE University, that are proving highly effective in training a modern workforce. But in this chapter, our touchstone is sensitive dependence on initial conditions. So, instead, let's address preschool, elementary, and intermediate education.

Let's address preschool, secondary, and intermediate education.

---

28 Steve Jobs Commencement Address, June 12, 2005, http://news.stanford.edu /2005/06/14/jobs-061505/.

29 Ibid.

30 Ibid.

Here's the model that's been in evidence for nearly one hundred years: build massive physical structures. Hire administrators and teachers. Have all of the students leave their homes, trudge or be bussed to these physical structures, then wade through a full day of lecturing and testing. Lather, rinse, repeat, over and over, day in day out.

Why? Today, with all of the technology in our midst, with all we've learned about how children, tweens, and teenagers learn, why are we still relying on such a structured, inefficient, way too expensive, and in many ways constricting model? To me it makes no sense that, instead of rethinking the model, we throw even more money at preserving the status quo.

Let's not get in to why we are where we are. Instead, let's ask, if we could start from scratch today, how would we educate our children? Consider:

- Less full-time staff; fewer "jack of all trade" teachers; more part-time "specialist/evangelists."
- Business and society cooperate: companies allow specialists with outstanding skills to volunteer as teachers perhaps five to ten hours a week.
- Dedicated classrooms become as-needed lecture halls, lab facilities—or whatever is needed.
- The classroom becomes more virtual; students "meet" maybe only twice or three times per week—if that often.
- Videoconferencing leverages the expertise of top-flight teachers; guest lecturers can more easily participate "from anywhere."
- Lectures/lessons are recorded and can be viewed/repeated on demand.
- Technology better tracks individual performance, helps tailor personalized instruction.

Even Elon Musk is getting in on this realization; that, with today's technologies, we need to rethink education. The executive, known for his innovations not only for electric vehicles and spaceships but also AI and neurotechnology, is investing in XPRIZE, a group focused on creating new learning models to deliver better education to the Third World. Could it be Musk is meanwhile delivering some sort of message that the US Department of Education, National Education Association, and teachers' unions should heed?

In the end:

Education matters.
Encouragement matters.
Risk-taking matters. Inspiration matters.
Purpose matters.

But the difference between the developed world and the emerging world is exactly this: in the developed world, the baseline is much higher than where folks start in emerging worlds. It is very, very hard to forge a successful life if where you start is a war-torn place and your schools are closed for months on end—for example, those children born and reared in Baghdad since 2002.

We cannot go so far as to insist that education is a right; just as we cannot go so far as to demand that everyone be born to wealth, prosperity, beauty-pageant looks, and world-class athleticism. But we need to be vastly more aware that initial conditions matter—and to think about what can be done to help level the playing field wherever possible.

Most of this effort requires awareness and capital—we must be willing to invest in the poorest among us, those starting from the least beneficial initial conditions.

But, at the same time, we must also be evangelical. Initial conditions matter. But so does personal responsibility. If the world owes each of us a job, then what responsibility does each of us bear beyond showing up, clocking in, and then collecting our pay every two weeks?

> We must be willing to invest in the poorest among us.

The developing world needs fundamental investment in better education, health, and initial conditions. But here in the developed world, part of the education required is to help workers realize: it's not that business and capitalism are bad and government is good, though there is most definitely a sub-culture in this world that preaches this. And the truth is, such attitudes suppress the individual's ability to unleash their own entrepreneurial capabilities. The earlier we can reach children's minds to instill them with this mindset, the higher each can climb from where they currently reside, regardless of their initial conditions.

■ IN PRACTICE

- Not everyone has the same gifts—but do we owe it to society to ensure that even our least capable members are trained in ways they can consistently and reliably earn some basic standard of living?
- Even if we do recognize the need for a basic living standard, what commensurate steps, if any, should still be taken to drive greater personal accountability?
- When evaluating candidates currently possessing similar skills and attributes, doesn't it make sense to also compare initial conditions, if only as a means of evaluating fortitude/drive?

A safety net can come from family, friends, government, and most assuredly from the financial practices of the employer.

SAFWAN SHAH

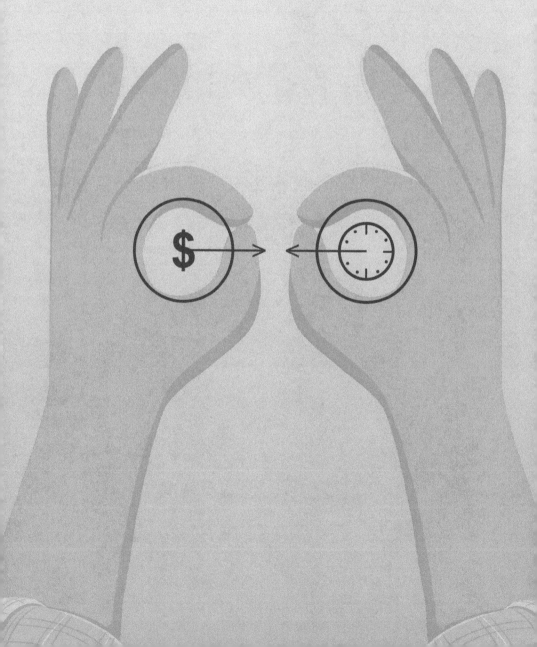

Perhaps our ten fingers led to our counting system.
Perhaps pi is not the most frequently used constant.
One constant in the life of low income employees:
"Is it okay to pay now?"

SAFWAN SHAH

Chapter Six

The Pi (π) of Paying

Defining our perimeter: the remarkable occurrence and application of constants

- *The magic of 10: its role in behavioral finance*
- *Ten can help or hurt us: a 10 percent variance can deliver immense pain or profit*
- *Time, crickets, and constancy: my early foray into artificial intelligence (AI), and what I came to understand about time's role in the human condition*

⬛ ⬛ ⬛

In my PhD program at the University of Colorado at Boulder in the early '90s, I encountered this remarkable, decidedly eccentric, but eminently likeable character, Rajan Mahadevan. Google his name and you'll learn that in 1981 Rajan earned his place in the Guinness Book of Records by reciting, from memory, the first 31,811 digits of the infinite, irrational constant we all know as π.

One day I asked Rajan, "So how do you do this—memorize so many figures?"

For starters, Rajan is gifted with a brain that is in some ways better optimized than most for rote memorization of numerals. For his family, realization of this reality fully germinated when, at a birthday party at age five, he went out into the parking area and memorized the license plates of the attendees' vehicles.

But by no means do such natural talents—such initial conditions—imply there is no further work to be done. Memorization of this magnitude requires focus or, more specifically, as in this case, mnemonics. For pi in particular, Rajan explained, "I like to use cricket scores/summaries." So, for Rajan, numerous strands of six, ten, or even eighteen digits of pi's first thirty thousand or so simply coincide with the outcomes/statistics of past cricket matches and players. Of course, a few other memory-supporting coincidences are also in the chain, perhaps some phone number or address plus someone else's birthday, but you get the idea.

So, Rajan and I became friends and we would talk about pi, cricket, or even on occasion our respective work. But then he moved to Florida to work on his PhD in cognitive psychology or something similar. And my other friends and I always mused: is this more a case of Rajan heading to Florida to study other people's brains; or did the people in Florida bring him there to study his?

Defining our Perimeter

So, what is pi? Appropriately derived from the Greek word *periféreia*,
pi is nothing more than the ratio of the circumference of a circle to its diameter. Basically, multiply a circle's diameter by pi and learn how many units of measurement are required to complete a full revolution. Child's play? Yes and no. Simple, yes. But the irrational nature of this constant has attracted the fascination of mathematicians throughout the ages. Archimedes, for example, couldn't precisely define the value of pi, but he was able to draw its boundaries.

Today, the value of pi we use within our calculations is often a matter of tolerance—just how precise do we need our answer to be? For our precision laser-cut turbojet fan-blade designs, we might move four or five or even seven digits beyond the decimal. For estimating how much soil we'll need for those raised planting beds we're planning in the backyard, 3.14 might do.

Meanwhile, for interplanetary navigation, Marc Rayman, director and chief engineer of NASA's Dawn Mission, says there's no need to go beyond just fifteen decimal places (3.141592653589793). Assuming, say, a circle with a 25 billion-mile diameter, fifteen decimals would result in errors no greater "than the length of your finger."[31]

So, why bring up pi in the first place? For starters, constants help in our research, analysis, and understanding of the world around us by reducing the

> So, why bring up pi in the first place?

moving parts in an equation. Having a constant means that there is one less variable to worry about, like substituting "c" for the speed of light—3.00×10^8 meters or 186,000 miles per second. Note that without c being a constant, there would be nothing so elegant as $E = mc^2$ helping us describe our universe.

Another important aspect of pi is that it doesn't matter how big or small the circle happens to be, the ratio between circumference and diameter is always pi. This "invariance" of ratios is a powerful tool we can use in all walks of life: the ratio of fat mass to lean mass for dieticians and personal trainers; the ratio between arm span and height for predicting the performance of would-be recruitment picks for college basketball, baseball, or football coaches; or any of a number of financial ratios for CFOs/controllers and other executives.

Even marketers dream of identifying constants that, once converted to an effective tag line, can inspire customer loyalty. I often wonder, can we say "Every Day Low Prices" is a constant used in marketing for Walmart?

The Magic of 10

Pi, along with many of the other observable constants in our universe, is just so elegant. Pi is so perfect, recurrent, and inviolable—much in the same way as so many other constants revealed in nature by mathematics. Today, for example, I stand in wonder of the Fibonacci series, the continuous logarithmic chain long referred

---

31 "How Many Decimals of Pi Do We Really Need?" EDU News, March 16, 2016, https://www.jpl.nasa.gov/edu/news/2016/3/16/how-many-decimals-of-pi-do-we -really-need/.

to as the golden ratio that defines structures as diverse as seed heads, flower petals, hurricanes, and spiral galaxies. If you will, each number in the Fibonacci series is the sum of the previous two numbers (1, 2, 3, 5, 8, 13, 21, 34, . . .).

And so I wonder, are there similar constants in behavioral finance we've yet to deduce? Maybe nothing so precise as pi or the Fibonacci series or even Planck's constant—the independent thoughts and actions of individuals aren't quite as controllable as other relationships in nature—but something that might still be useful?

And as I embarked on this personal journey, over the years combing through sources such as various credit agencies, the US Census, and my own anecdotal experience, indeed, something keeps surfacing: the number 10.

For instance, one of the things I observed is that the average credit card debt per household—that's the total debt on all credit cards they have in their possession—ranges from around $4,800 to $5,800. Now, compare this to the average household income of around $57,000 a year. It's not precisely 10 percent, but, goodness, we're close, so let's dig a bit further.

Next, look at the average salary of those we call low income—it's around $38,000 or roughly $3200 per month. In concert, look at the average value of checks cashed at check-cashing kiosks and big-box retail outlets—it's $320 or, again, roughly 10 percent. Then what's the average value of a payday loan? Again, it's around $300 or, again, 10 percent of the monthly earnings for the low-income family.

So, what is it about 10? Is it the numeral? Even if we switch from base 10 to base 2, it's still elegant: 1010.

Want to induce someone to sign a contract? We don't offer a discount of 6.6 percent, 7.4 percent, or even 9.8 percent—it's 10 percent that inks the deal. Ever see a sign at the grocer saying, "this week only: 7.7 percent off tomato juice"? It's 10 percent that screams, "Time to buy!"

> It's 10 percent that screams, "Time to buy!"

Looking to buy a house? A price that's 30 percent higher than your initial budget will probably mean: no way. But if it's only 10 percent more, many buyers will sharpen their pencils and move ahead with the deal regardless.

Jack Welch meanwhile tells us that the golden rule in turnover for an optimized workforce is to rid the business of its bottom 10 percent, the lowest-performing employees, each and every year. (Dare I say, however, perhaps a company could avoid this latter need through more effective hiring and development?)

Why is 10 so prevalent and so attractive to us? It could be no more complicated than the fact that we have 10 fingers. According to George Ifrah, speakers using Central Africa's Ali language use the term *moro* to represent both the number 5 and a human hand. Moreover, the word *bouna* means the number 2, and is combined with *moro* to form *mbouana*, the Ali word for 10. So literally, 10 is two hands. Based on this and related inferences, Ifrahs goes on to say, "It is therefore very probable that the Indo-European, Semitic, and Mongolian words for the first ten numbers derive from expressions related to finger-counting."[32]

No, it's not scientific. Yes, there's a significant degree of variance. No, it's not always a percentage but sometimes just a numeral. Still, it appears to me that when it comes to matters of personal financial consequence or benefit, credit decisions, payment terms, or even sales prices, the number 10 seems conspicuously, behaviorally influential as well as omnipresent.

> The number 10 seems conspicuously, behaviorally influential as well as omnipresent.

Ten Can Help Us or Hurt Us

Ten creeps in to numerous other aspects of behavioral activity, often with a positive impact. Our fitness coach tells us: just 10 more sit-ups or pull-ups or laps in the pool, and it sounds to each of us, certainly, like we can go that much further. Or dieticians say a healthy weight loss is around 2 pounds per month. In turn you

---

32 Georges Ifrah, *The Universal History of Numbers: From Prehistory to the Invention of the Computer* (New York: Wiley, 2001), 22.

must burn 3,500 calories to lose a pound of weight, whereas the average person today consumes about 2,500 calories a day. So, to hit the target 2 pounds per month, we create a 250-calorie deficit or,

We can comprehend 10; we can achieve 10 more of nearly anything.

in other words, a 10 percent daily reduction (30 days × 250 calories = 7,000 calories = 2 pounds). Again, we can do that. We can comprehend 10; we can achieve 10 more of nearly anything.

There's even a beneficial 10 in commercial credit terms: 2/10 net 30 means pay this invoice within 10 days to get a 2 percent discount (or pay the full amount within 30 days). Or when a typical middle-class wage earner finally decides to get their financial affairs in order, they don't say, "From now on, I'll save 6.2 percent of my gross," but instead, "I'll start saving 10 percent of my take-home."

But 10 may also be hurting us—particularly the least well-off among us. A sales person can use 10 against us, understanding they can often close the deal by saying, "Okay, here's my final offer: 10 percent off." A car salesman can offer a discount of up to 10 percent of the sticker price without further approval—often enough of an illusion to clinch the sale. Ten can be used against us as a powerful influence.

As discussed earlier, make a 10 percent error as a wealthy person, buy too much, take on too much debt or whatever, and it will be easy to absorb and recover. But the same 10 percent mistake or loss can have a devastating effect on the working poor. We've also spoken about how stress can lead to less rational decisions. But let's combine this with the stress that comes from being poor in a wealthy society. Speaker, writer, and professor of behavioral economics at Duke University Dan Ariely, says that "the capitalist system is basically designed to create things that tempt us."[33]

Meanwhile, the poor are continuously exposed—via social media,

---

33 "3 Scientifically-Backed Strategies to Help You Reduce Temptation," Cornell Tech, November 24, 2015, https://tech.cornell.edu/news/3-scientifically-backed -strategies-to-help-you-resist-temptation.

film, television, etc.—to how "good" others have things. "Imagine living in a doughnut shop, but you cannot have a doughnut yourself," says Ariely. Eventually, mistakes are made. The poor buy something they want but cannot afford. And now they're in over their heads.

And how do they make such mistakes? Imagine being hungry for hours on end—a full sixteen hours without a meal. Now, just before bedtime, your choices are that salad or that one-third pound fast-food burger with a side of fries. Calorically and sensually, you are at the margin. Or we've gone for ten years with a regular television, and that fifty-inch high-definition flat screen at the rental center—costing just 10 percent of our monthly take-home pay—soon enough becomes too tempting to resist. When we go for so long without having something we need or crave, sometimes the level of desire leads to bad choices.

And now, once they've made a single 10 percent mistake, they will often be tempted to make yet another mistake, taking on a payday or title loan. Now they are locked into a repeating cycle, where 10 percent of their earnings every two weeks is being docked to make up for the prior 10 percent loss. Now, they are on a treadmill.

So, when it comes to issues such as credit usage, payday loans, and check-cashing services, is 10 a coincidence or a conclusion? Are these organizations conducting detailed data analysis and then steering financial matters to some optimum ratio—optimum for the providers, mind you, not the end users? Truth be told, this is increasingly likely, as it is in such groups' interest to develop the optimum means of monetizing their customer. We would need an honest response from such providers themselves to be certain, but in the interim it seems to me that 10 percent continues to harm the working poor.

Time, Crickets, and Constancy

A big piece of my PhD research was around conducting experiments to record the communication of a large number of neurons. A neuron fires electrical signals called spikes at a rate or frequency that is not understood at all. These spikes are electrochemical in nature, and the actual process through which they are generated is well understood. What is unknown is what these signals mean, signify, imply; are they random, relatively unintelligible or purposeless phenomena, building blocks of a massive communication network, or just a means for synchronization—or even something else?

Now of course, we (like many before us) suspected these spikes must be understood if we were to ever understand how the brain actually communicates. In this context, my focus became a search for detecting patterns in the firing sequences (spike trains). The hunt for a neural code, an alphabet. It could be the timing, or perhaps the size of the spike, its amplitude, or both in combination.

Fortunately, one doesn't need to plug into living human brains with over 100 billion neurons to hunt for these answers. There are many simpler and much easier ways to acquire nervous systems when it comes to analyzing modes and methods of communication. I used crickets (*Grylloidea orthoptera*). Not only were they readily available at pet stores, but their central nervous systems were virtually untouched by evolution for nearly 250 million years, making them simple in form and thus nearly ideal for our work.

The research itself, my PhD thesis, was titled, *Analyses of Biological Nervous Systems Using Artificial Neural Networks and Fuzzy Logic Techniques*. The work was novel for at least two reasons. First, this was one of the early attempts to capture over fifty nerve cells firing patterns simultaneously. But perhaps of even greater interest was that, in doing so, we had to utilize methods and tools that today would be instantly recognizable as early-stage artificial intelligence (AI).

Observation; development of hypotheses; experimentation: these are essential to basic research. But to make sense of all of the data we were collecting, I had to immerse myself in neural networks and AI. So, for three years, nearly every day and night, I became consumed in trying to understand nonlinear math, feedback control systems, various complex algorithms like backpropagation, unsupervised learning, and so on. But, in doing so, I was privileged to have access to some amazing people like Paul Smolensky (today the Krieger-Eisenhower Professor in Cognitive Science at Johns Hopkins University) and Michael Mozer (a professor at UC Boulder's Institute of Cognitive Science).

Just how difficult is it to identify order amid the chaos of neuronal signals? One way I've tried to explain things: imagine an alien life form investigating the planet Earth and its inhabitants. Their only source of data gathering is a recording instrument they've managed to establish that can tap into the sounds—collisions, applause, lulls, music, etc.—of a major football stadium. Armed with only this data source, how difficult would it be for these aliens to detect what is going on in this stadium, let alone the outcome or score?

What I've just described is very much akin to the hunt for a neural code. What we learned is that every cell has a certain time series pattern. Moreover, using an array of AI techniques, we found different kinds of cells had patterns that differed from other kinds of cells. And we found we could cluster these groups in such a way that the ratios between the times the various sets of cells were "spiking" to each other were highly correlated. In any case, what we inferred was that cells, by spiking at different times, were generating a code that could be received and understood and thus could indeed be influencing the activity of other parts of the organism.

> Just how difficult is it to identify order amid the chaos of neuronal signals?

But, in order to be consistently effective in coordination/communication, wouldn't it follow that these primitive pulses would need to have consistent meaning, that their timing would need to be precise? And so, time-based constants are evident even at this fundamental level in neurobiological systems.

And, as I think about this today, I begin to realize that time is in fact a constant for us all. We can live our lives any way we choose, and we can do whatever we like in any given day, week, or month—our actions are our own options. But however we live our lives, time continues.

Of course, our perception of time is variable. As Einstein describes it, a hand on a hot stove for a moment seems an eternity, but, when a man sits in a room talking with a pretty girl, an hour seems like only a minute. This is how time must seem for the low-wage earner: hours that pass slowly for relatively little reward. In this sense, poverty may create the sense of an extended life of torment.

So, time is a constant for poor and wealthy alike—as is "10" in its various incarnations. The trouble is, for the poor, both of these constants are less a source of benefit and more a treadmill or source of angst.

▪ IN PRACTICE

- Constants help to create certainty and understanding within the interaction of key variables: so what constants have been identified by your industry? By your company?
- To what extent are you using AI to develop such insights in your own business?
- Are time-based businesses using data to maximize their monetization/exploitation of lower-wage earners/borrowers—developing optimal "constants"?

"Yes, it is okay to pay now, and I can." That's okay by me!

SAFWAN SHAH

> For the millions of employees living paycheck to paycheck, the calculus of time and money is a constant, never-ending burden. They have only their time, which has so little leverage over money.
>
> SAFWAN SHAH

Chapter Seven

Time and Calculus: Putting Time to Work

Time, Newton, and Leibniz: understanding the beauty of calculus and its illustrative capabilities, shedding light on our everyday experiences

- *Time, bandages, and nice girls: time and relativity in our daily existence*
- *Who controls time? Who chases time? Understanding how our role in society and business drives our span of financial flexibility*
- *In Time—or the relative value of our time*

⬛ ⬛ ⬛

Ticking away,
The moments that make up the dull day . . .
PINK FLOYD

Workin' nine to five,
What a way to make a livin',
Barely getting' by,
It's all takin' and no givin' . . .
DOLLY PARTON

I only have an hour and a half.
RACHEL SALAS, *In Time* (dir. Andrew Niccol)

■ ■ ■

We all experience time. But depending on financial circumstances, perceptions of time vary dramatically.

Think about velocity. Velocity equals the instantaneous change (delta or *d*) in some other variable (*x*) given a corresponding instantaneous change in *t* or time. For this, we write:

$$\text{velocity} = dx/dt$$

So, what is this *x*? It could be a point on a graph depicting a physical location: our vehicle moves through a given plane, hence, velocity equals how far we've moved relative to that point, divided by how much time has elapsed.

> Some people's time spent at work accrues vastly more wealth than others'.

But we could also use *x* and *t* to denote our earnings over time. And, without forming any equations or doing any math whatsoever, we understand, intuitively, that some people's time spent at work accrues vastly more wealth than others'. Conversely, by comparison, other people's time earns relatively little.

Leave it to Adam Smith, Hans Rosling, Milton Friedman, and other economists to explain variations in employee earnings; what we want to discuss are relative differences in the perceptions of time.

Time, Newton, and Leibniz

Let's begin with a short shout-out to Messrs. Newton and Leibniz for our enhanced quantitative understanding of time. For centuries prior, our computations were static; frozen in time. We could calculate *this* much mass or *this* much height.

But, with *differential* and *integral* calculus in our toolkit now, we can obtain a far deeper understanding of how time impacts our world. And, while controversy continues regarding who should get credit for what based on when, both Newton and Leibniz are generally credited with the development—or, it could be said, the discovery—of calculus.

How Far and Fast?

With *differentiation*, Newton's forte, we are able to calculate derivatives, leading not only to velocity (the first derivative) but also acceleration (the second derivative). Differentiation, you may recall, shrinks events and, more precisely, their functions into their most infinitesimal increments. Thus reduced, we are then able to evaluate not only motion over time but also instantaneous motion.

Newton's *Philosophiæ Naturalis Principia Mathematica*, published in three volumes beginning in 1687, was an absolutely incredible leap forward in mathematics and physics. Among other accomplishments, Newton introduced methodologies that advanced Kepler's three laws to an exponentially more rigorous understanding of planetary motion. Kepler had used observations to develop an empirical understanding of the movements of matter through space.

Newton, however, posited a new concept, gravity, and then instead of using measurements developed formulae and the methodology of calculus to explain the interrelationships between proximate heavenly bodies. And again, into all of his calculations, he introduced time, an absolutely essential and insightful gauge.

How Much?

Leibniz also dabbled in both time and space while creating/discovering calculus, and, in fact, is given credit for developing much of the notation still in use today. But many consider his area of greatest contribution—his forte—to have been the *integration* side of calculus.

Integration, you'll recall, is the process of summarizing all of that space beneath Newton's differentiating curves. It's a means of measuring the amount of "stuff." And Leibniz is particularly well known for his creation of cutting-edge mechanical calculators such as the pinwheel and arithmometer.

Time also comes into play within the relatively confrontational relationship between Leibniz and Newton. In 1684, Leibniz published his masterwork, *Nova Methodus pro Maximis et Minimis* (roughly *Methods for Maximization and Minimization*), a paper describing a wide range of calculus techniques he had been developing for a decade or so. Newton, however, could lay claim to similar work as early as 1666—work that could easily have been seen to be every bit as revolutionary as Leibniz's own ideas, though never published formally.

Thank the Plague

Looking back, most observers give the benefit of the doubt to Leibniz—indeed, historians say it is likely that his version of calculus was developed largely independently. Moreover, consider these two key quotes from Newton:

> I stood on the shoulders of giants.

> If I have done great things it's because I was standing in the closet of smart men taking notes and then publishing their ideas as my own.[34]

As such it might seem likely that others—not Newton himself—would be the ones fanning the flames of this "who was first?" controversy.

But, in keeping with our theme, it should be noted that time itself played a key role in the development of calculus. It was thanks to the plague-driven closing of Cambridge in 1666 that Newton had so much free time on his hands. That time, spent contemplating matters as mundane as the falling apple, led to many of the breakthroughs we now call Newtonian physics.

---

34 Isaac Newton, *The Correspondence of Isaac Newton: Volume 1, 1661-1675* (Cambridge: Cambridge University Press, 2008), ed. H. W. Turnbull.

Time, Bandages, and Nice Girls

Dan Ariely is an Israeli psychologist and a pioneer in behavioral economics whose books are excellent. I also enjoyed a presentation of his in San Francisco not long ago. One of the stories he tells involves his own experience of being badly burned in an accident, so much so that his entire body seemed to leave him absolutely mummified—covered in bandages from head to toe.

As a result, his body's core defenses—his antibodies—were absolutely devastated. To fight infection, the doctors and nurses were forced to remove his bandages and clean and salve his wounds every two to three days.

Now, imagine the pain of removing such a dressing from even a minor cut or surgery of your own—it tends to give anyone trepidation. And what strategy do we tend to take in such instances? For most, I'd wager, the choice would be to get things over as quickly as possible—that is, to use the least amount of time. Most of us would grab one end of the band aid or sterile pad, grimace in anticipation of something painful, then pull all at once.

Ariely's entire body was covered in severe, raw, and still seeping wounds. So, the doctors and nurses attending to his wounds, trying to help him get through the ordeal with as little suffering as possible, would pull the dressings off as quickly as possible.

Fast-forward to clinical research being conducted by a professor at Columbia. Detailed research into burn treatment and recovery had proven the importance of slow removal of such bandaging. Slow removal, it turns out, does far less damage to recovering tissues, speeding recovery and reducing scarring. And once that information got back to the clinic where Dan Ariely had been treated, all were likely devastated by the news. They had done their best, thinking that the amount of time spent suffering was the most important variable.

Who Controls Time?

Let's think about a sole proprietorship—we'll call it Jimbo's Juice Hangout. Now Jim likes to think of himself as "decent people," conducting business ethically and trying to treat everyone fairly and equally. In terms of what actually happens in Jim's business, various actors have more or less leverage in terms of when and how they get paid, depending on who they are and what role they play.

Pay Me Now

Jim's rent for his commercial space requires a three-year lease along with a three-month deposit, and is paid one month in advance. Due the first of each month, Jim pays this expense with clockwork precision.

Jim's vendors, the folks who bring him fresh ingredients like strawberries, blueberries, and bananas? They're a precious lot—in demand by so many farm-to-table establishments and restaurants—that they can demand to be paid on delivery. The same goes for the suppliers who provide ancillary items like paper cups, plastic spoons, and napkins. So, indeed, Jim keeps his checkbook or cash on hand and pays his vendors the same day. In the event that he chooses to pay thirty or sixty days later, there are additional terms and a commensurately higher price he must pay.

> Paying workers in arrears provides a significant source of working capital.

As for Jim's retail customers, they may pay by cash or credit card, *as and when* they buy. This means they're required to pay for their heirloom blueberry/apricot frappes at the register, before any "juice-ista" throws a single ice cube or dash of freshly drawn coconut milk in the blender.

And now what about Jim's team of workers? Those wages are paid two weeks in arrears. Why? Well, that's just customary in the business world. And for a small business like this, where Jim writes his own paychecks right out of cashflow, this paying workers in arrears may temporarily preserve some of his working capital.

Still, how much capital preservation are we talking about, if Jim allowed his employees to access a portion of their earned wages prior to payday? Let's say, in the middle of a pay period, six of his ten employees request an advance of $400 or half their already earned wages. How much would financing $2400 cost Jim?

Since the cash for his payroll has to be held in liquid funds, the best he might hope for is a money market rate of around 1 percent. So, the net benefit to Jim of withholding this much cash is a mere $24 a year—minus taxes!

The question becomes: Jim, why—in a world where everyone else gets paid on demand or has terms—would you make your employees wait to get paid? Why in particular would you cause so much financial stress and create so much difficulty for your workers, when the actual financial cost of paying more often is almost negligible and helps them better serve your customers?

> The actual financial cost of paying more often is almost negligible.

Jim is a business owner. Jim bears far more risk than his employees, for certain. But, simultaneously, Jim no doubt has daily cashflow plus greater cash resources and credit as well as experience and capacity for risk-taking. His employees, on the other hand, are likely counting on their cashflow to make immediate ends meet.

So why not pay out from earned wages when an employee is desperate, stressed, and likely to end up paying a late fee or get hit by an overdraft? In Jim's case, it may be a simple matter of keeping matters organized and streamlined. An on-demand payout would initially mean slightly more paperwork, until automated, but for the employees it could mean peace of mind, higher engagement, and significantly better quality of service. Surely Jim would be a more successful employer if his employees were less stressed about their personal lives and more focused on their customers. In no way is Jim worse off. He still remains in control, while his employees also feel they have a semblance of control. A classic win-win.

The World's Largest Piggy Bank?

A quick visit to Bankrate.com tells us that, with deposits of over $3.6 trillion at the time of this writing, the largest bank in the world is the Industrial and Commercial Bank of China (ICBC). This is a regulated institution, strictly defined as a bank.

But, using a looser definition of banking, my own nominee for the world's largest bank would be the cumulative bank of the world's employers. Its deposits? The aggregate sum of each employer holding at least one week of salary before payout, and most employers holding two weeks of salary at any given time. Assuming a per capita income of $1000 per week for 75 million hourly workers, this would add up to a staggering $75 billion waiting to get paid by the end of each week and $150 billion by the end of the second week. Not a small bank by any means. But is this imaginary bank making money while holding on to employee funds? To understand this matter, we need to look at how payroll is managed and processed.

> My own nominee for the world's largest bank would be ADP, the world's leading provider of payroll services.

Meet ADP, the world's leading provider of outsourced payroll services and for twelve years named as one of the most admired companies by Fortune magazine.

In 2017, ADP processed payroll of one in six workers in the US and had seven hundred thousand employers as customers. Add to this the fact that the majority of employees are being paid either one or two weeks in arrears, and that adds up to a lot of cash. On average, in fact, ADP has about $20 billion dollars in accrued earnings available for deposit each night.

Remember Jim? Because he pays his employees by check out of his own business account, Jim gains the value of this delay or float—that enticing $24, before tax, each year. But larger businesses have many more employees, thus potentially amplifying the value of this float. And who earns the interest in the case of larger businesses that outsource their payroll? The answer: deferred employee earnings are paid currently to ADP and similar providers. And so instead of the companies themselves earning the entire interest on this float, a portion of the value flows to ADP.

> Every economic activity is based on a hierarchy of time. The entity with the greatest leverage in any given commercial situation is the one who controls and monetizes the time involved.

Of course, this cash is very carefully managed, invested only in short-term, lowest-risk instruments. Average interest is around 2.2 percent. But the point is that companies themselves are not gaining any significant value from this float. Instead, service providers like ADP bundle the associated earnings on behalf of employees and earn that 2.2 percent interest on that $20 billion dollars as an offset to their own operating costs. It's one of the components of their total return, which can be taken into account when determining pricing. And since payroll processing is a competitive field, all competitors are continuously seeking to offer greater value for less cost—otherwise, providers would merely pocket the interest, raise their fees, and think no more on the subject.

In this way, the float on employee earnings helps to subsidize payroll processing service fees to the tune of about $440 million dollars every year, earned off employee wages that have yet to be paid. Moreover, these circumstances mean that payroll processors and their small/medium/large customers are the ones in control of the timing of payments to employees.

Time: Some Control It; Others Chase After It

Every economic activity is based on a hierarchy of time. The entity with the greatest leverage in any given commercial situation is the one who controls and monetizes the time involved.

The realtor/property owner seems to have the most leverage, demanding not only up-front rent but also a security deposit. Vendors, though able to extract payment "at the time of delivery," have slightly less control. Business to consumer (B2C) retailers—like Jim's juice place or any supermarket, clothier, or big-box store—are also able to demand immediate payment.

Others tend to chase after time. B2B sellers often extend credit to corporate buyers as a means of winning sales. Again, the larger the business, the greater the leverage.

Then there's the case of employees—those with the least leverage in the competition for time. In spite of what the Torah, the Bible, and other "good books" suggest, for the sake of their employer's bookkeeping convenience and the payroll provider's precious, income-producing float, workers will have to wait two weeks for their compensation.

Something else to note: those who control time often use their power against those who are chasing it. Those who are indebted, whether it's a car loan, credit card, mortgage, or payday loan, are carefully measured by those holding "the paper." Pay a day late? Here's a late fee—the Fin-Tax again. Pay more than a few days late, and we will activate an even higher, punitive interest rate.

> Those who control time often use their power against those who are chasing it.

Moreover, those in control of time can also "ding" your credit history—a signal to others with lendable resources to charge low-income families even higher rates. Chasing time is a less-than-ideal pastime for the relatively well-to-do, but it can be an absolute nightmare for the ones that can least afford it—our lower-income workers.

The Evolution of Time and Commerce

A modern, sophisticated understanding of time may be a relatively recent phenomenon, historically, but humans have been attempting to get more done in less time for centuries—since the beginning of civilization, actually. Most associate the assembly line with Henry Ford—who in the twentieth century so optimized time and space to produce one completed vehicle every thirty-five minutes. But even in twelfth-century Europe, a major city-state was mass-producing specialized masts, mechanical parts, rigging, and other provisions in what today is called the "Venetian Arsenal."

As society has become more advanced, personal time has become more valuable. People driving their mass-produced cars no longer felt they had time to sit down, order a meal, and enjoy matters in leisurely fashion. Perhaps sensing as much, in 1940, the McDonald brothers opened the first of what would eventually become a vast empire of fastfood restaurants bearing their name.

Humans have been attempting to get more done in less time for centuries—since the beginning of civilization, actually.

The McDonald brothers developed what they called their "Speedee Service System"[35] as a means of ingredient staging, pre-order preparation, and task specialization. Their system not only accelerated service, which was popular with customers, but slashed labor costs as well.

And soon, a milkshake-mixer-salesman-turned-franchise-rights-owner named Ray Kroc would rely on this system to turn the McDonald's restaurant into the global enterprise it is today. Again, time proved profound, because it was only Kroc's astonishment about the fact that a single establishment would need eight of his mixers—enough to produce forty-eight milkshakes simultaneously—that prompted his interest in the budding chain in the first place.

Note also that it was about this same point in commercial history—the late 1940s/early 1950s—when Taiichi Ohno and Eiji Toyoda initiated the principles and practices that not only supercharged the production of Toyoda products but also became the far broader just in time (JIT) production revolution. It should come as no surprise that conference rooms in my office are named "Just in Time" and "Real Time"!

Fast-forward to Sears, K-Mart, and others: Why shop at one source for shirts, another for shoes, then yet another and another for hardware, a television (they didn't say "electronics" in those days), furniture, stationery, or toys?

---

35 Christopher Klein, "McDonald's Surprising Start, 75 Years Ago," History.com, http://www.history.com/news/hungry-history/mcdonalds-surprising-start-75-years-ago.

Not to be outdone (but rather, to disrupt), next came Walmart. The group so values its customers' time that, in addition to all of the services just mentioned, let's also add groceries—one less stop for busy consumers. Moreover, Walmart did away with the traditional limited-time-only sale ("Get here this weekend or you'll miss out on our bargains") and instead based their retail business on the principle of "everyday low prices."

Something that might not be so obvious to someone standing in a Walmart checkout line, the true genius behind the company's low prices has to do with the timing of its logistics. Walmart squeezes every conceivable moment of waste out of its logistics and shelf-stocking processes so as to speed the pace at which merchandise moves through the supply chain and into customers' hands. Speed—time—is the very essence of the Walmart model, and the primary source of the company's epic rise.

> Next up in history's constant battle to save time is Amazon.

But let's not rest on our laurels just yet. Next up in history's constant battle to save time is Amazon. Largely blamed for the demise of the traditional book store or music seller, today Amazon is threatening virtually the entire brick-and-mortar retailing world. And with the acquisition of Whole Foods, CEO Jeff Bezos now has his company's sights set on revolutionizing the grocery industry.

And how does Amazon produce such dramatic disruption? It improves the customer experience and accelerates its sales by eliminating *time* from the buying process. Moreover, the most sophisticated sellers, like Amazon, are now using computers to anticipate their customers' needs, often before customers recognize them on their own.

Those who know what we want before we do? Surely, they are masters of time. The success of Amazon's Echo, as well as many other "virtual assistants," is based on discovering ways to capture and accelerate sales by giving consumers the means of making their purchases in real time. Are you about to run out of milk? Just say it out loud, "Alexa, order milk," and all will be taken care of. Immediately.

Amazon's overarching line of thinking: by taking control of time for the customer's benefit, we will also benefit. This is being similarly pursued through ease of searching and access; through auto-replenishment, next-day delivery, same-day pickup points, and (soon) drone-based same-day delivery. Walmart—and now Amazon—are among today's penultimate examples of time-based competition. It is their mastery of time—both theirs and their customers'—that drives their commercial advantage.

The Relative Value of Time

Think back to our second chapter. If there is a primary cost to the batch process, this cost can also be thought of in terms of time. How much is time worth to you? To society? The amount of time we spend waiting for batches to process is something we can easily calculate mathematically.

Consider what your life would be like if your kitchen ran in batch mode only, delivering meals precisely at nine a.m. and nine p.m. Think about the evening meal, for instance, if it meant always going to sleep right after your dinner. You would be less healthy, you wouldn't sleep as soundly, and you would likely develop high blood pressure.

Your landlord? He eats when he likes—because he gets paid in advance. The distributor gets paid upon delivery. We all compete to save time for our customers. But what about the employee? Pricing power rests with those who own time. And from what we know of how we treat our employees, it is clear they have little control of time.

Of course, certain employees have greater leverage in terms of their value to our organizations. These will be the relatively higher-paid workers and, in some cases, the handsomely compensated executives. Such employees, those with commensurately

> Pricing power rests with those who own time. And from what we know of how we treat our employees, it is clear they have little control of time.

greater resources, are also greater masters of their own time.

The well-to-do don't need to take time for an eleven-hour drive when they go from Houston, Texas, to Atlanta, Georgia—they fly. And the even more well-to-do don't need to waste time waiting for a commercial flight—their time is so valuable they will rely on a private jet. The very essence of being well-to-do involves leveraging time: their food is cooked for them and served to them; they have executive assistants and valets; they're driven by others from place to place so they can use the time to work en route.

> The very essence of being well-to-do involves leveraging time.

Those whose time is so valuable they will pay extra to conserve it can also afford to receive their pay two weeks in arrears. Such individuals and families have enough of a cushion that they aren't waiting for their checks to arrive before they can spend again.

But, for the working poor, that two-week time interval—that cushion of time that earns Jimbo's Juice Hangout a paltry $24 per year, before tax—can be truly priceless.

There's something deeply ironic and (to me, at least) quite disturbing in the reality that time is so precious for the very workers whose time is *least* valued by their employers.

In Time

In spite of its ravaging by the critics—scoring a mere 35 percent on the Tomatometer (Rotten Tomatoes)—*In Time* is a film I very much enjoyed and whose story arc is in line with the whole of this chapter. We don't want to publish any spoilers here, but the basic plot is of a society where time becomes a fungible currency. People exchange "life"—time—for goods and services. The wealthy have accumulated so much time that they practically command eternity; the poor are at all times living on the cusp, scraping, clawing, and fighting for every remaining moment.

Within this construct, a society that buys and sells everything in units of time, there is a scene that never fails to stir my emotions.

A woman of meager means, Rachel (played by Olivia Wilde), is racing to catch a bus to get home to see her son (Will—played by Justin Timberlake). Boarding, the bus driver informs her that the fare has risen from one hour to two—it costs two hours of life to ride the bus to her destination. Paraphrasing the scene from my recollection, it continues:

Rachel   *"But it's always been just one hour."*

Driver   *"Well, now it's two—the price went up."*

Rachel   *"My son is meeting me—he'll pay the difference."*

Driver   *"Sorry, can't do that—against policy."*

Rachel   *"Please, it's a two-hour walk—and I have only one and a half hours left."*

Driver   *"Then you better run!"*

Who knew that a Justin Timberlake movie could provide such poignant commentary on the ideas of Newton and Leibniz?

▣ IN PRACTICE

- How and where does time play a role in your business? Are you competing based on time? Are you offering your customers better use of their time?
- Are you using this same "time-based" thinking when thinking about one of your greatest assets: your workforce?
- What sorts of steps could you take to enable your workforce to make better use of its time, both "on and off the clock"?
- How much of your cashflow is "locked up" in batch payment processes? Would it yield greater returns in your hands, the hands of the payment processor, or in the hands of your workers?

> The "time" in our lives can be a burden, or just a feature in our landscape.
>
> SAFWAN SHAH

"

Our relationship with time is evolving rapidly; the impact on your low income employees is magnified by its scarcity; they don't have the income to buy time.

SAFWAN SHAH

Chapter Eight

In Time, We Find Lucy

Society is experiencing an inflection point—a "Lucy" event

- *Our relationship with time—our "life rhythm"—is undergoing profound transformation*
- *Discovery and time: consider the sixteenth century's eBay*
- *What "task" is it? Instead of time, we consider tasks*
- *The rise of the machines: dystopia or paradise?*
- *Let's not leave anyone behind!*

❧ ❧ ❧

In 1974 Ethiopia, when two hundred bones (about 40 percent of a skeleton) of one *Australopithecus afarensis* were discovered, many anthropologists believed they had found the long-sought "missing link" between apes and humans. In particular, researchers were excited about her "valgus" knee, a sort of knock-kneed characteristic that indicated an upright gait. Those scientists closest to the discovery were so impressed with this "individual" that they gave her a name inspired by a Beatles song written by John Lennon and played often at the excavation site: Lucy.

But what—or who—exactly is this missing link? Creationists reject evolutionary theory altogether, which is fine by me. I'm not mentioning Lucy as some foregone conclusion but rather as a concept, a marker for a profound transition, a moment where we went from zero to one.

I want to leave the world better off than it was when I found it.

I care about Lucy because she embodies a kind of inflection point. And I don't know about you, but in my own life I'm continually on the lookout for any sort of inflection point, if for no other reason than that I want to play a role in helping advance society. I want to leave the world better off than it was when I found it.

And, to my mind, we are living through a "Lucy moment" right now. Today's Lucy moment involves how we deal with time itself.

The Rhythm of Time

In contributing to our understanding of time, Herr Leibniz also provided greater insight into how time impacts the human experience. If you haven't noticed, I'm a tremendous fan of music and lyrics. So was Leibniz, as evidenced by one of his keen insights: "Music is the pleasure the human mind experiences from counting without being aware that it is counting."[36]

Music takes place in time. Earlier, we referenced Merle Travis's "Sixteen Tons," Pink Floyd, and Dolly Parton. To this growing list of time-themed compositions, let's also add Cher's "If I Could Turn Back Time" (written by Diane Warren). And, while we're at it, I must confess that I am also a huge fan of electronic music. Why? Because its timing is simply captivating; I find it energizing and entrancing.

As Leibniz understood so well, our minds and our bodies are well-attuned to counting, whether we are aware of it or not. After all, when a musician hears the beats of the metronome—tic, tic, tic—they are emphatically linking music to time.

But something about time is changing; in terms of our internal clocks, something profound is occurring. The "speed of life"[37] seems to be accelerating, as technology enables all things to occur faster, better, and cheaper. A focal point for this is the internet,

---

36 "Why a course in the Mathematics of Music?" Mathematics of Music, https://www.ams.jhu.edu/dan-mathofmusic/.

37 "Speed of Life" is also the name of an instrumental-only tune by David Bowie.

whose own rhythms, pitches, scales, and decibel readings are increasingly the heartbeat and soundtrack of our existence.

Initially a research and later a business tool, the internet is now intertwined with all phases of our lives. We not only bank and shop online, but we now go there to create as well. We store our work in the cloud—collaborating simultaneously with whomever else is permissioned in our workspace. We socialize virtually, sharing our lives on Facebook. Time—and space—no longer matter; we are always connected. In fact, this book is being drafted using Dropbox to share files back and forth between me and my collaborators.

One of these collaborators is my close friend Don Peppers, co-author of *The One to One Future* as well as other great works. Don told me he remembers being witness to a step change in the speed of business life in early 1989. He was in New York working for the ad agency Chiat/Day, which handled the Apple account. Every employee at the agency had an Apple computer on their desktop, and in early 1989 the agency went "live" with a new electronic mail system, enabling workers to send detailed messages to each other without printing out any paper

> Disconnecting is supposed to deliver Zen-like calm. Instead, in today's reality, disconnection increases stress.

and without having to visit someone's office or trying to coordinate the right time for a phone conversation. As Peppers recalls, "I immediately detected an incredible acceleration in the velocity of business. We all felt it."

Fast-forward to the present. Feeling as though there's just no respite from the stress and immediacy of email, Peppers recently told his wife, "that's it, I'm going to take off an entire weekend without checking my 'in' box."

Come Sunday evening, however, Don was neither blissful nor meditative. Instead, his psyche bordered on a state of panic as he realized that an important client discussion had been taking place over the weekend with no participation on his part at all. And his deliberate radio silence had been interpreted by some of his colleagues as tacit assent for an idea he really didn't agree with. Moreover, by the time he finally checked his email, his inbox was so packed that it took an hour just to read them all, let alone respond.

Disconnecting is supposed to deliver Zen-like calm. Instead, in today's reality, disconnection increases stress. The internet is both a manifestation and conductor of our accelerated lives and work. We have no choice today but to struggle to maintain pace with its rhythm and tempo.

Discovery and Timing

When I think about economic history, I have no doubt whatsoever regarding the absolutely critical role played by pure luck and good timing in terms of determining success or failure.

Not all that long ago, I learned about Pierre de Montaigne, brother of renowned Renaissance author Michel de Montaigne. The latter you may know as the father of the "essay." Michel, in the later years of his life, penned (literally quilled) a series of contemplative musings on such key issues as "questioning everything," "doing something no one has done before," or "letting life be its own answer." In doing so, Michel introduced or perhaps merely was the first to succeed wildly with a first-person writing style that remains popular and effective today.

His sibling was no slouch either. In the late 1500s, brother Pierre de Montaigne proposed that each town in his region of France should set up a plaza or other meeting place where people could "post" their wants and needs:

> I want to sell some pearls; I want to buy some pearls. So-and-so wants company to go to Paris; so-and-so is looking for a servant with such-and-such qualifications; so-and-so wants a master; so-and-so a workman; one man this, another man that.[38]

---

38 Sarah Bakewell, *How to Live: A Life of Montaigne* (Other Press, 2010), 48.

Had there been a sixteenth-century internet—and had Pierre been willing to apply the needed elbow grease—this idea might have attracted both early and late-stage investors eventually evolving into what we now know as eBay. So, in commerce as in life, time's advance may be inevitable and unavoidable, but its impacts are mercilessly indifferent.

Pierre and I share something in common: we each had a great idea or two that fell victim to lousy timing. For example, in 1998 I had the notion to leverage this new massively communicative internet into an online university. I started writing my own insightful and intuitive calculus course that was to be rendered using this wondrous program we had created (the adjectives are my own, not necessarily those of more objective sources).

> So, in commerce as in life, time's advance may be inevitable and unavoidable, but its impacts are mercilessly indifferent.

The trouble was, our demo just didn't work because, at that time, only leading-edge web users had enough bandwidth. The internet was just too slow.

Of course, all businesses have to adjust with the times. When first conceived in 1997, Netflix took on Blockbuster and the rest of the home movie rental business by making it easy to use the mail to rent physical DVDs. But then, as more and more homes added more and more high-speed internet, the model shifted, circa 2007, to streaming video.

Around 2006 I recall visiting this vast—at least for the time—data center in Santa Clara (Silicon Valley). Arrayed in the back were twenty or so of what I recognized to be very powerful and very expensive EMC storage servers. Naturally, I wondered what kinds of companies or businesses were aligned with all of this cutting-edge technology, but I soon spied a small red slip of paper with some information on it. Curious—perhaps some would say nosy—I pulled it within range and saw that some 80 to 90 percent of this computing power was under contract with Netflix.

Looking back, I now realize that this was in fact the point in time that Netflix began putting its nascent net-streaming services through their trials. Soon, anyone would be able to watch whatever they liked whenever they liked. Appointment television was already on its death bed; streaming, on-demand television, movies and gaming would soon nail shut its coffin. I was witnessing a Lucy moment—an entire industry was about to experience time-based disruption.

What Task Is It?

Our perceptions of time are shifting so fast that many of us no longer ask "what time is it?" but rather "what task is next?"

The day begins. Your calendar is no longer on your desk—awaiting your arrival following coffee, a commute, and likely more coffee and a bagel. Instead, your calendar is on your phone, which is also your alarm clock, rolodex, flashlight, and road map to anywhere—not to mention video camera/camera, and "will call" for theater tickets and boarding passes.

Before you fell asleep, your phone told you what your next task would be and what time it should begin. More than likely, it was upon this basis that you decided what time to rise. Then throughout the day, your phone or your tablet/laptop/desktop bleeps at you that there is just ten minutes to go before your next task begins.

> Our perceptions of time are shifting so fast that many of us no longer ask "what time is it?" but rather "what task is next?"

In today's world it is the task that drives us. Join a call; feed the cat; pick up Mom; write that report; board that flight. We are desperately attempting to achieve greater control of our time by focusing more acutely on what it is that needs to be done. New technologies have delivered us into a world in which watches have become auxiliary pieces of jewelry; it is our devices and their calendars that now tell us what we need to be doing and when we need to be doing it.

A major part of this shift involves time becoming more and

more illusory; it is much more relative than before. Like me, dear reader, you are probably a business executive—or can relate to a similarly time-driven role. So, I ask you to now try and visualize how our own perception of time, as business executives, differs from the perception of a lower-paid worker. You might start by simply comparing the task list of a relatively well-to-do business executive with that of a janitor, or a call-center agent, or a caregiver in a retirement community.

The well-to-do have *many* tasks to complete, and economics would suggest that the time of the well-to-do is considerably more valuable. They are probably well-to-do in the first place because they create more wealth in any given moment than most other people do—people who are less skilled, or less endowed with capital or other advantages.

And much of a well-to-do person's existence involves delegating relatively lower value-added tasks to others. They may have an administrative assistant helping to manage access to their online calendars—only those worthy of "my" time need apply. They will likely be involved in strategic planning or managing client relationships, while the nuts and bolts of any workflows are delegated to lesser-paid staff—people whose time has less value.

The well-to-do are far more likely to have a housekeeper (no time for cleaning, laundry, or grocery shopping), a cook (nothing microwaved in this house), a lawn maintenance provider for mowing and leaf raking, and/or a nanny (who has time for diaper changing?). Time is money—and the well-to-do will pay money to save time.

And, of course, the more time they save, the more value they can create, and, in turn, the more money they can make—giving them the option to enjoy ever-greater, more costly leisure activities. They will eat more often at restaurants (quality food prep takes time), and they will fly to their destination

Ironically, however, the more options we have, the busier we actually feel, because every time we decide to do something now, we have to decide *not* to do so many other things.

rather than driving there or taking a bus. The more wealth at one's disposal, the more options one has for spending one's time.

Ironically, however, the more options we have, the busier we actually feel, because every time we decide to do something now, we have to decide *not* to do so many other things. Thus, even though a well-to-do person is actually quite free to indulge in a variety of relaxing pleasures, they will nevertheless have the illusion of being quite busy, with little time for all that they would very much like to have time for.

Further down the economic totem pole, time is just as compressed: No matter where an hourly worker puts in the hours, and no matter what task they are being paid to accomplish, their employers are almost certainly applying every possible productivity metric—while almost salivating at the thought that these tasks, too, may one day soon be automated. But the less well-off worker has no maid, no personal assistant. The less well-off among us cannot afford to eat away from home, much less to fly off on vacation.

So many tasks to perform—cooking, cleaning, caring for the children, traveling to and from work—but so little time. In the modern world, time is task-oriented, but the well-to-do have far more options for deciding which tasks they will tackle and which they will offload to others. The well-to-do will still view time as a precious asset (because there are so many things to do!), but it is an accessible asset that can be replenished and expanded simply by spending the money required to buy more of it from others, whether that be a maid, a nanny, or a personal assistant.

But, for the hourly worker—for the clock-punching clerk, janitor, caregiver, or maid—time is just as precious; it cannot, however, be so easily replenished. So, the well-to-do control time; others chase after it. But, as the speed of life accelerates, the latter almost never catch up.

> The well-to-do control time; the others chase after it.

The Machine Era

History has seen many great epochs; numerous "Lucy moments" of profound change, ranging from the Yucatan asteroid that likely ended the Jurassic era, to the Industrial Revolution that ended the agrarian era. Today, many see the rise of the machines—of robots, AI machine learning, and related technologies—as symbolic of a new era arising. Indeed, it is machines that most will associate with this new epoch, but fundamentally it is time and our perceptions of the passage and value of time that is experiencing the most profound change.

Indeed, today we are experiencing a Lucy-like moment with respect to our relationship with time. And as "machines" build ever-greater footholds within our assignment of essential tasks, this particular Lucy moment now poses an existential threat for a vast swath of low-skilled individuals. That is, many are about to see the commercial value of their own time dwindle into relative nothingness.

I "hear" the argument, but it's nothing we haven't heard before. A simple question: There are millions of homes with gardens, but how many jobs have been taken away by lawn mowers? My belief is that, as low-skilled jobs disappear, others will take their place. If there is any great net loss of low-skill opportunities, then humanity will respond, taking steps such as implementing basic universal income. There may be some upheaval, but ultimately, humanity will cope, finding new uses for human labor and resetting its time- and value-based parameters.

> Many are about to see the commercial value of their own time dwindle into relative nothingness.

But there is another fear—a deeper-seated fear—surrounding the rise of the machines. Indeed, many leading thinkers are broadcasting warnings of a coming technological singularity. Humans themselves can be jealous, vindictive, vengeful, tribal—even fanatical. So, what happens when "our" robots become self-aware? Will they act on our worst traits?

We have developed more ways to destroy one another than ever before, But, at the same time, humans have an immense capacity for being kind and doing good.

Recognize the Manichean nature of humanity. Certainly, today we have developed more ways to destroy one another than ever before, ranging from ICBMs carrying nuclear devices to drone-delivered bacterial weapons. But, at the same time, humans have an immense capacity for being kind and doing good.

Moreover, while there is more automation today than ever before, despite what headlines and twenty-four-hour-a-day news might lead many to believe, violence and killing is at an all-time low. As Steven Pinker writes in "A History of Violence,"

> The decline of violence is a fractal phenomenon, visible at the scale of millennia, centuries, decades, and years. It applies over several orders of magnitude of violence, from genocide to war to rioting to homicide to the treatment of children and animals. And it appears to be a worldwide trend, though not a homogeneous one. The leading edge has been in Western societies, especially England and Holland, and there seems to have been a tipping point at the onset of the Age of Reason in the early seventeenth century.[39]

History is in fact replete with examples of great acts of kindness, benevolence, and compassion. So my point is: even if in time we ever do manage to create an ultra-intelligent being, it is probably more likely to devote itself to acts of amazing good than it is to pursue evil. In short—I do not fear AI, but rather welcome its arrival as yet another tool for improving the human experience.

---

39 Steven Pinker, "A History of Violence," *The New Republic*, March 19, 2007, https://newrepublic.com/article/77728/history-violence.

Those Left Behind

But there are concerns. In this Lucy moment, where the very essence of time is in flux, we need to make certain that all of humankind benefits from our greater sophistication in understanding and managing time.

I've often admired as well as contemplated Dali's seemingly time-distortion-focused painting *The Persistence of Memory*. Depicted clocks are molten, misshapen. Certain scholars said that no doubt this was Dali's riff on the new theory of space-time relativity. But according to other sources, Dali dashed such enlightened observations, saying that his images were more akin to "Camembert cheese melting in the sun."

But to my thinking, Dali's melting clocks represent a perfect metaphor for understanding our relationship with time. To me, the Lucy moment has arrived, and humankind is now set to have a profoundly more intricate relationship with time. We are no more in control of time than before, and yet we are mastering it.

> Time is being controlled by fewer and fewer people.

The trouble is, time mastery is only taking place at one end of the wealth spectrum, so time is being controlled by fewer and fewer people. As the speed of life accelerates, the few at the top are able to cram more value and living into every moment, while those at the bottom find themselves running ever more frantically just to keep up.

We *must* open our eyes to this circumstance, this dilemma. We *must* begin taking steps to enable more people to control their own lives, their own time.

■ IN PRACTICE

- Your workers have much on their plate, robbing your business of potential productivity: are there any steps you might be able to take, any services you can provide, that might lead to mutual benefit?
- How are your customers experiencing time in new ways?
- Do shifting perceptions of time present opportunities for disruption in your industry—and are you the likely disruptor or the disrupted?

*Juggling is a hell of a lot easier if you don't need to keep
so many balls in the air, let alone axes and chainsaws.*

SAFWAN SHAH

When we re-imagine the world of our customers and the world of our employees, do we summon our better angels?

Chapter Nine

The Savage Capitalists Meet Corporate Social Responsibility

Giving consumers—casino gamblers and drug users—just what they want ("despicable" me!)

- *Times change: the rise of the socially conscious consumer*
- *Conscious Capitalism: to what degree are businesses culpable when it is their customers who are making the bad decisions?*
- *Emerging research demonstrates: by doing good, companies often do well*
- *Achieving long-term, sustainable value creation*

■ ■ ■

Thank you industrialization. Thank you steel mill. Thank you power station. And thank you chemical processing industry that gave us time to read books.

HANS ROSLING, Economist (whose recent passing we all mourn)

Companies must ask themselves: What role do we play in the community?

LARRY FINK, Chairman and Chief Executive, BlackRock, Inc.

■ ■ ■

Let me reassure you first and foremost, dear reader, that I am a fan of capitalism and business. Never before in the history of the civilization—of commercial and societal interactions and contracts—has there ever been a stronger force than capitalism for increasing global prosperity and improving the health, well-being, and general standard of living for everyone. There. I'm on record, and I hope that message is clear.

At the same time, however, there is no question in my mind that capitalist business executives everywhere have noticed the increasing drumbeat of consumer consciousness. Consumers are paying more and more attention to environmental, social, and governance (ESG) issues; and they focus acutely on corporate social responsibility (CSR). Investors are following in lockstep. Not only are there now many published ESG and CSR indices but also another set for socially responsible investing (SRI).

And so, increasingly, the wise capitalist becomes keenly attuned and responds to this increasingly visible and more broadly demanding set of "deliverables." Deliver well on these issues—do so better than your competitor—and you create competitive advantage, you savage capitalist, you!

Despicable Me

Business profit can only ever be achieved by giving consumers what they want. Be it food and clothing, or prostitution, smoking, gambling, fatty foods, hard-core drugs, or bacon-stuffed, buttered baked potatoes: no one achieves success in the business world unless there's customer demand to be satisfied.

The very idea of starting and operating a business means doing something rather than nothing. Businesses exist because the owner is passionate, either about profit or about some vision of the future, or a desire to do something for others, or some combination. Businesses will succeed if and only if there are enough customers who want what the business creates. And yet a growing number of voices today ascribe nothing but evil intent to the providers of such products and services.

At this confessional, I will tell you that I worked as a technology service provider in the much-reviled brick-and-mortar gambling industry. Yes, I played a key role in helping casino patrons get secure access to their cash so they could play—eh, gamble.

Most people think that casinos simply cannot separate fools from their cash fast enough. On the contrary, the successful casino learns the optimum pace at which to separate the customer from their cashflow, because to do it too swiftly and too regularly without respite might cure the subject of their desire to gamble entirely.

But, of course, no entrepreneur sets out to be an evildoer. Initially, I had hoped to use capitalism to perform good works for humanity. In the late '90s, as the internet was booming, I and my partner—friend, really—had this bright idea to help customers by using technology to consolidate all of their different financial statements and provide data analytics and planning services to make the service sticky. Something like Mint, the popular service now owned by Intuit.

> Casinos simply cannot separate fools from their cash fast enough.

And, of course, it was our dream that consumers would value this service of consolidating financial records enough to pay for the privilege. So, we formed a company to make that dream a reality. We called our new company "Infonox," a play on "in Fort Knox" (i.e., secure).

Reality, however, was quick to set in. As we pitched our idea to potential investors, the conversation almost invariably went something like this:

Investor   *"So, you're an engineer, and your team, they're engineers, too."*

Infonox   *"Yes."*

Investor   *"So how much experience do you have in marketing? What's your track record in execution?"*

Infonox   *"Well . . . we are taking steps to . . ."*

Investor (interrupting) *"Yes, of course you are. So again, how many statements are people receiving?"*

Infonox   *"Well, six is about the average . . ."*

Investor   *"So, how much are they paying for the first statement?"*

Infonox   *"Well, nothing, it's free."*

Investor   *"So, how much are they paying for their second?"*

Infonox   *"Also free."*

Investor   *"Okay, what's six times zero? Never mind. But thanks for stopping by; oh, and be sure to have your parking validated."*

The door closed in our face repeatedly. But with no money in our pockets—persistent sorts were we—and so motivated, we kept knocking. Then lo and behold, we called upon just the right door at the right time.

Late '90s. Loads of personal financial data beginning to accumulate, along with the continuing evolution of AI tools beyond the primordial capabilities I had applied to analyzing the nervous systems of crickets. Now the tools were even more powerful, able to more readily trace and analyze patterns. You know who would love to dig in to such a pool of insight? You know who would *really* like to know everything there is to know about someone's finances with just a few mouse clicks? The casino industry, that's who.

> Now the tools are even more powerful, able to more readily trace and analyze patterns.

I had no experience in casinos. But I do like numbers. I imagined that, if I was smart enough to help figure out how to grow a tomato in space without being a gardener, or to get a cricket to tell us how organs and muscles communicate with the human brain, then maybe I could design a worthwhile experiment or two for the Las Vegas crowd.

So, here was my fledgling company, and one day we met with a group that was the operating partner in a joint venture that included Bank of America and First Data (the world's largest payments company at that time—they even owned Western Union). And they asked us to bring in our technology and have a look at one of their key issues: how to enable real-time check and credit card usage in a casino, so that casino patrons would always have quick and ready access to a wider swath of their financial resources. That is, if they want more cash to gamble, we'll do our best to make it happen instantly.

Just imagine being a penniless engineer like me, owning a company with zero products and only a team of hungry data geeks in tow. But now suddenly our motley crew is given access to virtually all of the payment data any casino can muster. We were like kids in a candy store, unleashing a sugar rush of capitalist creativity.

Over the next eight years, we invented many tools and innovations for the casino and payments industry. Our paramount achievement, the invention of which I'm most proud, was the world's first biometric ATM. That is, our ATM was a machine that could look at you, determine that you are in fact you (in the flesh, so to speak), and then cash your check or dispense your cash instantly. Now position such technological wonders throughout the casino floor, and you have a safe, reliable, and highly efficient mechanism for streamlining and accelerating the process of separating customers from their bank balances.

It was from the bowels of this beast—and please recall, I insist there is little shame in meeting the demands of customers—that I gained an even deeper appreciation for just how acutely focused businesses could be in shaving the most margin from the least wealthy in our society. Tapped out from what they had brought with them in cash and hoping to recoup their losses, gaming patrons by the score would gladly endure a shearing of 5 or 6 percent in transaction fees right off the top. Anything—just get us back to those levers, buttons, and blackjack tables as fast as possible.

And despicable, capitalist me? I was delighted to help such customers achieve their goals—both the casinos and their patrons.

> Just get us back to those levers, buttons, and blackjack tables as fast as possible.

Well, speaking on behalf of Infonox, my company before PayActiv, I can state unequivocally that, if you had your payment processed at a casino, there was a 90 percent chance that the casino was working our software or imitators of our software. Little old geeky early-stage AI-enabled Infonox. That is how deeply our products and services had penetrated casino payments processes.

Times Change

While conservative Benjamin Disraeli was running for the office of Britain's Prime Minister, it was suggested to him that he expose the fact that his liberal rival, William Gladstone, was in the midst of an affair. Upon consideration, however, Disraeli determined that broadcasting such information would actually bolster his opponent's standing. This was, after all, nineteenth-century England, where having a mistress would be viewed less as a disgrace and more as an achievement.

Disraeli reportedly stung Gladstone with a now-famous barb during one of their later discussions. Gladstone had leveled his own insult regarding Disraeli's character: "I predict, sir, that you will die either by hanging or of some vile disease." To which Disraeli replied, "That all depends, sir, upon whether I embrace your principles or your mistress."[40]

Though undeniably brilliant, according to the online source Quote Investigator, this exchange is more likely to have taken place between Samuel Foote, an eighteenth-century British actor and theater

---

40 "Benjamin Disraeli > Quotes > Quotable Quote," Goodreads, https://www.goodreads .com/quotes/93549-a-member-of-parliament-to-disraeli-sir-you-will-either.

manager, and the Earl of Sandwich. We can't know for sure because it was way before smartphones recorded everything for posterity.

But we digress. Our overarching point is that times change. There was a time in the United States where slavery was tolerated—including, as we mentioned, the indentured servitude sanctioned by senior government officials as a means of quelling rising prices for essential trades and crafts.

Smoking was also once a sign of sophistication, or masculinity, or (given the right "holder" and lighting) feminine sensuality. At one time, cigarettes were even considered healthy: A 1949 print ad featured the headline "More doctors smoke Camels than any other," with an accompanying movie theater commercial saying that time out for busy "men of medicine usually means just long enough to enjoy a cigarette."[41]

And consider the pace of social change today. Just a decade ago most would have thought the legalization of marijuana was still a long way off, while today it has been decriminalized in many jurisdictions, becoming a robust new industry in Colorado. Nor, a decade ago, would many of us have predicted the dramatically changed social attitudes toward homosexuality and gay marriage, and the liberalized view of all gender controversies that we see today.

> Consider the pace of social change today.

Times are also changing with respect to our attitudes toward socially responsible activities. More and more consumers really do care about issues of social responsibility. Just try to find a millennial, for instance, who isn't looking for a socially responsible job or career. Such values are now filtering in to choices about which brands, products, and companies consumers are willing to support.

Perhaps even more importantly, socially conscious consumers are better equipped than ever before in terms of the means of both collecting and distributing environmental, social, and

---

41 "Unbelievable: Doctors Recommend Smoking! 60 Years Ago," YouTube video, 1:12, posted by The Ad Show, March 5, 2011, https://www.youtube.com/watch?v=D-y_N4u0uRQ.

Socially conscious consumers are better equipped than ever before.

governance insights. Facebook, Yelp, Twitter—today there are numerous, highly-effective avenues for sharing and discovery. Whether someone is a full-blown activist or merely maintains a casual interest in such matters—odds are that any misstep by any product manager or company will rise immediately to the attention of "woke" consumers.

Conscious Capitalism

Do we have responsibilities beyond profitability, beyond returns to shareholders? In their book *Conscious Capitalism*, Whole Foods CEO John Mackey and coauthor Raj Sisodia write,

> Think of a business that cares profoundly about the well-being of its customers. Sees them not as consumers but as flesh and blood human beings who it is privileged to serve. It would no more mislead, mistreat or ignore its customers than any thoughtful person would exploit loved ones. Its team members experience the joy of service, of enriching the lives of others.[42]

Now think about how these ideas might apply to, well, I don't know—let's say the casino industry. Can a casino ever be a member of the Conscious Capitalism movement? Minimal investigation reveals to us that any major legalized gambling facility built over the last two generations is by law required to become a benefactor to its host community. It will be subject to special taxes to finance the building of schools, hospitals, and related socially responsible infrastructure—many on otherwise poverty-stricken Native American reservations.

---

42 John Mackey and Raj Sisodia, *Conscious Capitalism: Liberating the Heroic Spirit of Business* (Harvard, MA: Harvard Business Review, 2014), 31.

And, in the end, of course, casinos are merely catering to the desires of their marketplace, no different than Colorado's marijuana farms cater to theirs. Moreover, let's all admit that if it weren't for the regulated casino, these same customers would instead be placing their wagers with local bookies, or throwing dice in underground gambling parlors, and the only taxes being collected would be going to the organized crime operations that managed the business. (Note that the mafia isn't likely to provide counseling services for the gambling addicted.)

Moreover, even if you screw up big time in a regulated casino, emptying your own bank account and going in to more debt than you can possibly repay, as harsh an experience as this may be, it is still survivable. Screw up in gambling's netherworld, on the other hand, and you might expect to experience broken legs, missing fingers, and death threats leveled against family members.

So, in the value chain of the entertainment and leisure business, just where does a casino reside in terms of being a socially conscious/responsible enterprise? It certainly has a negative or two to contend with—particularly because it relies disproportionately on the less well-to-do for its revenues. But, on the plus side, it does provide entertainment for the masses and significant economic benefits, not just to its employees but to taxpayers. And, if we're going to close down the casinos,

Can a casino be a member of the Conscious Capitalism movement?

does that mean we should also shut down the many state lotteries? Just how many state and local governments rely on lottery revenue to fund their schools? Probably about the same ratio as there are low-income and far from financially savvy citizens who consider daily lottery picks as their version of a retirement plan.

But before we pass judgment, let's consider another industry or two. Think about the housing bubble, mortgage crisis, and economic collapse of 2008. Hundreds of thousands of citizens were buying more houses than they could afford, actively speculating that the housing market would rise, ensuring them a hefty profit in the future. Now, how exactly is that different from a casino? Isn't it true that home lenders, mortgage brokers, builders, and landscape architects are simply enabling a slightly more respectable form of gambling?

Businesses are just that, businesses, addressing demand.

The sophisticated technologies that underlie both the casinos and the financial markets that support home mortgages come from companies like IBM, Cisco, Intel, Oracle— and this list could go on and on and on. But does that mean that these companies are ethically compromised? Are these technology companies required to build schools and hospitals wherever they conduct business, held accountable for their end users? Of course not. Businesses are just that, businesses, addressing demand. And, in the final analysis, all demand comes from consumers.

Doing Well by Doing Good

In a report titled *ESG: Good Companies Can Make Good Stocks*,[43] Savita Subramanian, with Bank of America Merrill Lynch Global Research, writes that favorable environmental/social/governance results in enhanced returns. In particular, positive performance against ESG metrics has been shown to drive stronger long-term stock valuations. Looking at S&P common stock listings, Subramanian's work indicates that return on total equity is 5 percent greater among those companies with relatively higher ESG ratings. Moreover, any investor who purchased stocks with above-average ESG ratings [only] would have avoided 90 percent of the bankruptcies we've seen since 2008.

A follow-up report from the same research team and author finds even more support for the value of ESG investing. *In ESG Part*

---

43 Savita Subramanian, *ESG: Good Companies Can Make Good Stocks* (Bank of America Merrill Lynch, December 18, 2016), https://www.iccr.org/sites/default /files/page_attachments/equitystrategyfocuspoint_esg.pdf.

II: A Deeper Dive,[44] Subramanian writes that "ESG appears to isolate non-fundamental attributes that have real earnings impact: these attributes have been a better signal of future earnings volatility than any other measure we have found."

Not surprisingly, the number of investment funds and total assets under management (AUM) incorporating ESG into their criteria is skyrocketing. The BofA Merrill Lynch study, for example, shows that by the end of 2016 there were about a thousand such funds with total AUM of some $2.5 trillion. As Subramanian writes, "The idea that these concerns are just for tree-huggers is simply not true."

What drives this stronger long-term earnings performance among those with relatively higher ESG and similarly social consciousness imbued ratings? Consumers at large are demanding more from themselves and from the businesses they buy from. This also explains the rise of so-called benefit corporations or certified B Corporations—businesses organized with an expressly stated and relatively transparent and auditable commitment to community.

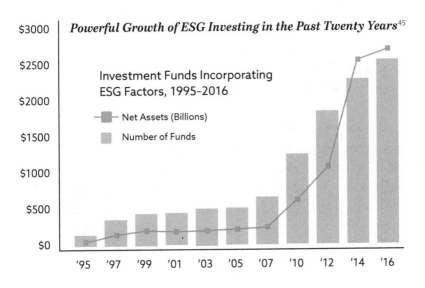

Powerful Growth of ESG Investing in the Past Twenty Years[45]

Investment Funds Incorporating ESG Factors, 1995–2016

Net Assets (Billions)
Number of Funds

---

44 Subramanian, *ESG Part II: A Deeper Dive* (Bank of America Merrill Lynch, June 15, 2017), 1, https://www.iccr.org/sites/default/files/page_attachments /esg_part_2_deeper_dive_bof_of_a_june_2017.pdf.

45 Subramanian, *ESG: Good Companies Can Make Good Stocks*, 10.

What Drives Long-Term Value Creation?

In a similar vein, businesses are increasingly finding it valuable and, in reality, absolutely necessary to focus more intently on the "long term." In his 2017 letter to CEOs, an annual exercise for the company, BlackRock Inc.'s CEO Larry Fink wrote, "companies must be able to describe their strategy for long-term growth. I want to reiterate our request, outlined in past letters, that you publicly articulate your company's strategic framework for long-term value creation."[46]

In full disclosure, note that Fink is pointing out that there must be far greater engagement between companies and their boards/shareholders. But, for even more acute context, note also that this chief executive from the world's largest asset manager (nearly $6 trillion in AUM) insists that any long-term focus must address a range of broader society issues. Again, according to Fink,

> Your company's strategy must articulate a path to achieve financial performance. To sustain that performance, however, you must also understand the societal impact of your business as well as the ways that broad, structural trends—from slow wage growth to rising automation to climate change—affect your potential for growth.[47]

Uh-oh. He's referencing all of that corporate social responsibility, environmental sustainability, diversity, and all other "virtual signaling" ideas we've been discussing. But the point he's making is that in today's reality all these buzzwords are becoming critical to true value creation and growth. That is, they are meaningful to the bottom line, now and in the quarters, years, and decades to come.

---

46 Larry Fink., "A Sense of Purpose," Blackrock.com, https://www.blackrock.com/hk/en/insights/larry-fink-ceo-letter.

47 Ibid.

As for timing, Mr. Fink's letter arrived in late January 2018, just as we were making edits to this writing. And forgive me for quoting here so heavily, but, in fact, his words are so in keeping with all that I had written that I feel they belong here:

> A company's ability to manage environmental, social, and governance matters demonstrates the leadership and good governance that is so essential to sustainable growth, which is why we are increasingly integrating these issues into our investment process.
>
> Companies must ask themselves: What role do we play in the community? How are we managing our impact on the environment? Are we working to create a diverse workforce? Are we adapting to technological change? Are we providing the retraining and opportunities that our employees and our business will need to adjust to an increasingly automated world? Are we using behavioral finance and other tools to prepare workers for retirement, so that they invest in a way that that will help them achieve their goals?[48]

In essence, capitalism itself is better served when it does more to address societal needs. Social benefits are merging, in other words, with consumer and investor interests.

---

48 Ibid.

▣ IN PRACTICE

- Can a business actually improve its performance by pursuing socially responsible goals?
- Are there customers who will gravitate toward your products and services once they recognize your "good" intentions? Are there customers who will defect if they notice otherwise?
- Is taking better care of your workforce a worthwhile goal of social responsibility?
- What easy steps are available—what simple things can you do—to make your business more socially responsible?

> I believe that we do make progress from generation to generation, for the most part, and I am excited to see a generation with more commitment to our better angels making its way through our society and culture.
>
> SADWAN SHAH

> Can "letting go" of the devotion to shareholder returns result in a liberated and better-performing workforce?

SAFWAN SHAH

Chapter Ten

Reimagining Products, Services, and the Planet

What's your story? Or, the importance of sharing your vision

- *Listen: your customers are telling you how to reimagine your business*
- *Dynamic intimacy means you know everything about your customers—and they know everything about you*
- *The machine age—a.k.a. the emergence of the Star Trek economy*
- *Workers of the world unite? Avoiding revolution is likely a simple matter, so do something about it!*

▦ ▦ ▦

The myth that profit maximization is the sole purpose of business has done enormous damage to the reputation of capitalism and the legitimacy of business in society.

JOHN E. MACKEY

▦ ▦ ▦

So, if capitalism is itself better served when it does more to address societal needs, what does this mean for the way a business should treat its workers and communities?

What's Your Story?

Successful businesses create and deliver products and services that meet the needs of their customers and prospects. Today, however, for an ever-widening swath of customers, that set of needs extends well beyond traditional boundaries.

Generally speaking, more customers than ever before have a conscious need to "feel good" about the products and services they are using. Certainly, they want products and services that attend to the basics: snacks that taste good; technology that gets the job done; airlines with comfortable seating, convenient flights, and on-time arrivals. But increasingly, consumers also want to feel confident that the businesses they support share socially "good" values similar to their own.

> More than ever, consumers expect everyone they buy from to treat workers fairly.

More than ever, consumers expect everyone they buy from to treat workers fairly, support civil rights, and respect the environment. But, in addition, socially conscious consumers want to support brands that treat women fairly, support LGBTQ rights, and, along the way, pursue a raft of ever-expanding sustainable business practices.

And the upside for businesses is that, for many consumers, buying from a company with similar values will escalate the customer relationship from a sense of quiet, personal satisfaction to an outright display of pride regarding the businesses the customer supports. Such consumers are becoming much more visible and vocal in terms of how they spend their money, including the vehicles they drive, the clothing they wear, the foods they consume, the performers whose concerts they attend, or the tracks they download: all "speak" to these consumers' sense of values and (watch out) social justice.

And, indeed, many such consumers go out of their way to broad-cast these ideas, not only by the decals on their bumpers or the logos on their jackets/yoga pants/backpacks but also through their social media posts, follows, up/down votes, or retweets.

The cynical among us might refer to much of this as virtue-signaling—the practice of competing for who can most visibly support "just" causes. For example, poking fun at Toyota Prius or Tesla owners for being more concerned with their social appearance than any true sense of wanting to save the Earth. Implying that Prius owners are essentially telegraphing their commitment to the environment as a means of propping up their own self esteem at the expense of others.

> Many such consumers go out of their way to broadcast these ideas.

But when we look more closely, it doesn't really matter whether or not some of the motivation for cause-related consumption is driven by the quest for status or appearance. The fact is simply that today these consumers represent a powerful force in the economy whose reach and influence will only increase. Regardless of the underlying consumer motives—and different consumers will have different motives as well as beliefs—business managers still want to ensure that their companies avoid any social consciousness missteps. That is, businesses need to take added care to make sure they "check all the boxes" to improve their position in social consciousness terms and, in particular, avoid any unnecessary mistakes driven by any lack of awareness or focus.

The savviest executives are doing all they can to listen even more carefully to these socially conscious consumers, trying to interact and engage with them directly whenever possible. Increasingly, the engagement process begins with storytelling. Your brand—your company, its products, and services—must offer consumers a com-pelling story. It has to be a story showing no effronteries to their world view: your company is not a polluter, it doesn't discriminate in its hiring practices, it uses energy and other resources efficiently.

But leading brands are taking this concept even further. They offer storylines that enable consumers to feel better about themselves and their socially conscious accomplishments. This product is 100 percent natural with zero artificial additives; ours was voted a "best place" to work in 2018; we subscribe to the industry-leading standards for 100 percent biodegradable packaging. Better still, our company is rebuilding the infrastructure of this tiny African town where our shirts are sewn—and pays a living wage, with free daycare and schooling for the children of its workers.

Dynamic Feedback

So, consumers and investors are ever more consciously and actively focused on doing "the right thing." But for a moment let's think more about why this is now the case. And one of the drivers here, in my estimation, is the arrival of an age of dynamic and continuous feedback and reevaluation, one that will only become more intensive.

> Consumers and investors are ever more consciously and actively focused on doing "the right thing." But for a moment let's think more about why this is now the case.

There was a time when commercial interactions were primarily personal. Communities were much more tightly knit—so personally connected that, if you bought a product and liked it, or disliked it, odds were strong you'd share that insight with neighbors.

Such intimacy also extended to commercial relationships. Not too long ago the shopkeeper knew your name, knew your family members, knew the products you preferred. Market research took place on a first-name basis. If something new came on the market, it wouldn't be long before the proprietor was able to collect all manner of direct feedback. Whether a product was a hit or a failure for local consumers, the shopkeeper knew why.

Moreover, there was likely a strong connection between said proprietor and the local sales rep for whatever products the proprietor offered in his store. The shopkeeper and the sales rep had ample opportunity to discuss the *hows* and *whys* of the monthly wholesale purchase of retail goods: "we'll take more of that, people love it; this, not so much." And, more than likely, the salesperson would pass along this information, either to some warehouse manager or directly to the manufacturer or importer or what have you. Data flowed intimately from ear to ear. It wasn't anything that a modern organization would consider "scalable"; but, as costly as person-to-person verbal interaction was, it had the advantage of being real. It was human.

As the Industrial Revolution continued to expand, however, this intimacy began to dissipate. Assembly lines whirred, large retailers began closing out mom-and-pop shops, and national brand reputations supplanted the personal trust that used to propel the shopkeeper's relationship with his customers.

It was in this environment that one-way mass communication—producer to consumer—began to flourish. This was the rise of Madison Avenue-style advertising. But, at the same time, the voice of the end customer grew faint, as feedback loops between manufacturers, distributors, and sellers grew longer and more muffled. Certainly, manufacturers could assess a product's value in the eyes of consumers by looking to broad indicators like aggregate sales, but this remained a relatively blunt-edged tool, failing to yield detailed insights. So, along came the product testing and evaluation industry with its focus groups, surveys, and the like.

> As costly as person-to-person verbal interaction was, it had its advantage of being real. It was human.

Fast-forward to the 1990s and the advent of the internet, not to mention advances in database and associated technologies so remarkable it might have surprised even Gordon Moore. Businesses could now collect, examine, and learn from vast caches of data.

But the internet was a two-way medium, ushering in a customer revolution. Now, consumers could "talk" not only to businesses but also to one another. The internet became more than just the reengineering and automation of yesteryear's intimacy; it was actually the beginning of something entirely new and exponentially more effective: computer-intermediated interactions with *millions* of customers, one customer at a time.

So, there is no coincidence as to why businesses are today paying so much more attention to corporate social responsibility or why socially conscious investing and business practices are today becoming so prevalent. And this phenomenon will continue to expand. More consumers are able to glean and share more information than ever before. Increasingly, they know how their products are sourced and what chemicals are being added. They know which companies invest in which nations and industries. And those that care know the multiples that company CEOs get, when compared to the wages of their lower-paid workers. In general, consumers are able to glean and share vastly greater information about the products they buy and the businesses they deal with.

Recognize: it doesn't matter whether consumer values/perceptions are in some way skewed or misguided. There is no monolithic worldview shared by all customers/prospects. For example, many agree with "competing" economists who argue that income inequality matters not one iota in the overall scheme of things; that today's proposed "solutions" to climate change will actually cost far more than the likely future net damages; that there is no gap in women's pay relative to men.

Still, issues of social justice tend to be taken quite seriously by those so inclined to virtue signal or, otherwise, to become outright activists. These individuals care deeply about such issues; they speak with one another across a range of platforms; and, where they can, they vote not only with their t-shirts, bumper stickers, placards, and megaphones but also with their wallets. They are a force to be reckoned with.

Listen, Reimagine

Your customers are speaking to you: louder, more clearly, in greater detail, but also with greater subtlety and more often than ever before. They tell you that, while they want improved products, they also want more socially conscious behavior from the companies they deal with. Are you listening?

Consumers' social consciousness signals are loud and clear. Survive for now perhaps by doing nothing; but, over the longer term, ignore it and you will perish.

As for new product ideas, note that today we are all product designers. Whatever you're selling, your customers are out there using your wares. They're speaking with one another about how well one product or service compares to this, that, or the other product or service. They're talking about what they like, what they don't like: what are the strengths and weaknesses of the various entries in the marketplace?

And, along the way, they are tinkering with things—doing things with your offerings you may not have imagined. They're out there innovating, customizing, and personalizing. Moreover, they're proud of what they're doing and more than likely are broadcasting their ideas on social media. By tuning in and engaging, companies gain access not only to an unprecedentedly powerful feedback loop, but also to a profoundly effective engine for product development and enhancement.

> Consumers' social consciousness signals are loud and clear. Survive for now perhaps by doing nothing; but, over the longer term, ignore it and you will perish.

Okay, let's now marry the new to the old. Many have heard about the OODA loop: observe, orient, decide, and act. This is a time-tested, frequently cited approach used by organizations to react to the events around them. But not everyone is familiar with its origin.

During my years as a graduate student developing experiments for a NASA lab, I learned about John Boyd, a fighter pilot during World War II and the Korean War. Boyd himself never once shot down an enemy aircraft—in Korea, for example, his role was as a wingman only. But it was Boyd who revolutionized air combat by becoming an evangelist for the idea that, by executing a continuous feedback loop, continuously, a pilot could stay ahead of, improve the odds against, and eventually defeat virtually any adversary. Boyd's concept of thinking continuously and critically based on the data available remains a key element of air combat training today.

As business executives, we must realize that, with the advent of cost-efficient, personalized, communication, we must do more to plug into this profoundly powerful crucible of product innovation, "imagineering," and disruption.

The Age of the Machines

Business intelligence systems (BI), artificial intelligence (AI), machine learning (ML), internet of things (IoT), distributed ledger technologies (blockchain/DLT): the emergence of these and related technologies can be expected to accelerate societal and commercial change at an exponential rate. But, for now, let's focus on the impact these technologies will have on the products and services that companies offer their customers.

Certainly, leaders are already harnessing such technologies to "listen" to customers and markets with astronomically greater effectiveness. Machines exhibiting deep learning and deep listening mean that companies can see and hear pitches and frequencies they may not even have known existed. As new patterns and new insights are revealed, businesses will access unprecedented product development and refinement opportunities.

> Think about all of the completely new products and services that will arise thanks to the machines.

Adding robotics means that companies will be able to design and produce new or enhanced products and services with little more than a few lines of code. Advances in 3D printing means the physical world can increasingly transcend time and space: any innovation created "here" can be instantly teleported—printed—"there."

Now, think about all of the completely new products and services that will arise thanks to the machines. Driverless, autonomous cars are an obvious opportunity. But what about all of the free time all of these drivers-turned-passengers will have on their hands. What productivity tools will they need? What entertainment will they want? Will cars need onboard kitchens? Seats that recline into sleepers? Game consoles?

Technology will also deliver nearly endless options for improving the human experience. From my own desk, I once pitched an idea for a personal intelligent assistant (IA): I called it the Mobile Valet, or "MoValet." The idea was to create a virtual assistant that could become a force multiplier for any individual. Talk to the MoValet; answer some questions; "teach" it about your current capabilities and your aspirations for the future. Who would you like to emulate? I think I was inspired by the famous Microsoft advertisement "Where do you want to go today?" and thought that every person should be able to get that question answered.

As the device learned, it would begin offering advice and assistance to help you reach your goal, whatever that goal happened to be. It's time to make this call on a project for work, or perhaps time to weigh yourself again and, depending on the result, go to the gym.

My vision was that the device would feature various crowd-sourced applications that I dubbed Movlets. These Movlets could be designed to help train the host/user in areas of interest or need. A key goal is to be able to retire by age seventy-five (reasonable for a millennial?). Whenever appropriate, the Movlet would provide subtle suggestions: perhaps buy the minivan, not the Corvette; use a five-year, not seven-year, loan; perhaps invest part of that $20,000 bonus, rather than splurging on a trip to Barbados.

Movlets could also be engaged to execute essential tasks. Find us the best price for this product; or choose a flight option that optimizes my work demands and leisure wants. And Movlets could even perform outreach. That is, your well-trained Movlet could interact with the similarly conditioned Movlets of others to share information—discreetly, of course. But the app could seek out others with similar needs or interests. Looking for pickup soccer in your area? Or maybe a compatible partner for a dinner (short term) or a life together (long term)?

Okay, so it was just an idea; it wasn't pursued in earnest. I seem to recall a wise person once telling me that ideas are plentiful; it's hard work and follow-through that drive success. That said, I cast MoValet into the ether of opportunity, although I do admit that I am waiting eagerly to see someone build a business around autonomous bots that would augment our day-to-day lives.

> Ideas are plentiful; it's hard work and follow-through that drive success.

You get the point: we are standing on the precipice of unparalleled change. When seeing the first steam-powered engines, few could have predicted the vast impact that the Industrial Revolution would have on the entirety of human civilization. Similarly, as they sent and received their first emails while clicking—often flirting—through AOL and CompuServe chat rooms, few consumers, let alone business leaders, saw the full measure of the coming social and commercial impacts of the internet.

So, where do we stand today? It is indeed the Age of Machines. But, at the same time, it is also the dawn of a new era of amazing promise for humanity. The machines can make each of us better and more effective; they will allow us to become more self-actualized. Society itself? Fifty years hence, this could be a society of plenty: limitless, environmentally neutral energy; frictionless automation to address any day-to-day need; humankind freer than we can even imagine today—freed from the drudgery or manual labor; capable of exploring our highest pursuits.

Remember *Star Trek*? Captain Kirk or any crew member simply pushed a button, and whatever precise meal they desired would appear, hot and ready. Later, Captain Jean Luc Picard and his fellow travelers could visit their holodeck for almost any adventure imaginable—without leaving the ship. The only resource constraint was the occasional need to find more dilithium crystals—in series context, the relatively rare controlling agent needed for warp engines.

We might call this the *Star Trek* economy, where society has so many resources and wonders, people work not because they have to but rather because they want to. We're on our way there; and, no, as I have mentioned previously, I do not share the feelings of dread others have expressed about the loss of jobs or the dangers of AI becoming self-aware and turning on its masters.

Workers of the World Unite?

Still, there could be more than a few rattles and rolls during the coming transition. Consider the upheavals that took place during the shift from an agrarian to an industrialized global economy. But I am actually of the belief that, with so many highly evolved communication and feedback mechanisms in place—and with so many additional "machine-bestowed" resources at our disposal—humankind will actually manage things more smoothly and fairly than before.

More immediately, I look at what I've seen, where I've been, and what's happening all around us today, and I can't help but wonder, just how close are we to some flashpoint? Some threshold of terrible inequality, the point at which tension between the haves and the have-nots spills over into serious social unrest?

History has seen many such flashpoints. When I was in Greece in 2009, I stood at the Agora (the "gathering place") and looked up at the Acropolis, wondering about Socrates and so many others who stood and talked

> Consider the upheavals that took place during the shift from an agrarian to an industrialized global economy.

and argued on that very spot of land. Being there was a moving experience. You see, that day in 2009, the Athenians were protesting against the government, because the Greek economy was in a state of collapse. Democracy in action. At that moment, twenty-five hundred years of humanity seemed to have merged into one powerful experience. There are no words to encapsulate that emotion except to say that it was an imperfect democracy (or demokratia) then, and it is still an imperfect democracy now. Because, in the end, there's no such thing as a "perfect" democracy.

But Greece wasn't always a shining beacon of democratic civilization. Prior to the establishment of Athens as the seat of the republic, there had been drought, price-gouging, and hoarding—so much so, that there arose great hunger and then, soon enough, riots and fighting. The violent crucible that led the Athenian leader Cleisthenes to introduce a series of political reforms leading to demokratia—rule by the people—in 507 BCE.

Poverty, uneven distribution of wealth, deprivation: conditions like these have been igniting unrest and upheaval throughout time. Aristotle observed: "Poverty is the parent of revolution and crime." Thousands of years—and many revolts—later, Karl Marx proclaimed, "Let the ruling classes tremble at a communist revolution. The proletarians have nothing to lose but their chains."[49]

Still more recently, recall the Russian Revolution of 1917, with all of its violence and upheaval. Note in particular the words of writer Maxim Gorky: "I am especially [. . .] distrustful of a Russian when he gets power into his hands. Not long ago a slave, he becomes the most unbridled despot as soon as he has the chance to become his neighbor's master."[50] Even in the twenty-first century, we see civil wars in the Ivory Coast, the Sudan, Syria, and even in Venezuela.

No, I am not saying there is risk of imminent global revolution; there are no guillotines being erected in the village squares throughout every developed nation. And, no, Madame Defarge is nowhere to be seen; there is no one quietly knitting the names of those they despise.

---

49 Karl Marx, *The Communist Manifesto* (New York: Simon and Schuster, 1964), 116.

50 Maxim Gorky, *Untimely Thoughts: Essays on Revolution, Culture and the Bolsheviks*, 1917-1918 (New Haven, CT: Yale University Press, 1995; trans. Herman Ermolaev), 95, https://books.google.ca/books?isbn=0300060696.

But consumers are on high alert. They are keenly aware. What I'm suggesting is that, by listening more intently across all frequencies and wavelengths, and paying attention to the long-term trajectory of society, your company can greatly improve its performance. At the same time, I'm also hinting that, by paying more attention to these issues, you might just be helping the world to avoid catastrophe.

So, avoid missteps by all means. And if you'll accept my frankest advice, do everything you can to be *fair* to the world—and that includes your own work force—noting that, at least sometimes, even the simplest gesture or action can deliver profound results.

◼ IN PRACTICE

- Ideas are everywhere—so how closely are you "listening" to your customers? To your marketplace? To your opportunity set?
- What business intelligence tools are you using to analyze your business? To scour social media? To gain insight from video/audio interactions?
- Remain a capitalist, but ask yourself: what more *could* you do to be fairer to your customers, to society, to your workers?

> *It saddens me to be at the end of this book and story, and it saddens me more to use such a visual cliché. But sometimes clichés are there for a reason; we can see the meaning instantly and understand it without ambiguity.*

SAFWAN SHAH

Every once in a while, a new technology, an old problem, and a big idea turn into an innovation.

DEAN KAMEN

Infinite players are not serious actors in any story, but the joyful poets of a story that continues to originate what they cannot finish.

JAMES P. CARSE

And, because it's worth repeating,

You can resist an invading army;
you cannot resist an idea whose time has come.

VICTOR HUGO

Acknowledgments

This book wouldn't have been possible without the inspiration of the entire PayActiv team. A special word of thanks to my cofounders Sohail Aslam and Ijaz Anwar.

To Don Peppers, Bill Millar, and David Carlick, I am deeply grateful for your insightful and thoughtful collaboration. To each one of you: thank you.

About the Author

An engineer by training and entrepreneur by accident, Safwan is the founder and CEO of PayActiv. After selling a previous company and committing to his golf game, Safwan pulled himself out of retirement to launch PayActiv and level the playing field for the financially vulnerable. Safwan's work connects the dots between math, economics, history, and music. His first book, *It's About TIME: How Businesses Can Save the World (One Worker at a Time)*, turns conventional wisdom on its head and calls for businesses to embrace the mantle of saving the world.

■ www.itsabouttime.io
■ www.timelyearnedwageaccess.com

ELEVATE HUMANITY THROUGH BUSINESS.

WE BELIEVE THAT BUSINESS IS GOOD BECAUSE IT CREATES VALUE, IT IS ETHICAL BECAUSE IT IS BASED ON VOLUNTARY EXCHANGE, IT IS NOBLE BECAUSE IT CAN ELEVATE OUR EXISTENCE, AND IT IS HEROIC BECAUSE IT LIFTS PEOPLE OUT OF POVERTY AND CREATES PROSPERITY. FREE ENTERPRISE CAPITALISM IS THE MOST POWERFUL SYSTEM FOR SOCIAL COOPERATION AND HUMAN PROGRESS EVER CONCEIVED. IT IS ONE OF THE MOST COMPELLING IDEAS WE HUMANS HAVE EVER HAD. BUT WE CAN ASPIRE TO EVEN MORE.

Excerpt from the Conscious Capitalist Credo. Read it in its entirety at www.consciouscapitalism.org/about/credo.

Conscious Capitalism is a paradigm that places people at the center of business. Conscious Capitalism, Inc. is an organization that brings businesses and business leaders on a conscious journey to elevate humanity through business by convening conscious capitalists, providing learning and development opportunities, and garnering PR for businesses, making the world a better place.

There are Conscious Capitalism events happening around the globe each week with over eighty conscious capitalist communities in twenty countries whose purpose is to connect with others, provide inspiration through storytelling, and give information and resources that allow community members to become stronger voices for business as a force for good.

We invite you, either as an individual or as a business, to get involved by joining us at a Conscious Capitalism event or a learning and development offering, and by sharing your story.

Learn more and join the movement at www.consciouscapitalism.org.

9 781950 466047